Translating Tradition

Peter Jeffery, Obl.S.B.

TRANSLATING TRADITION

A Chant Historian Reads
Liturgiam Authenticam

A PUEBLO BOOK

Liturgical Press   Collegeville, Minnesota
www.litpress.org

A Pueblo Book published by Liturgical Press.

Cover design and photo by David Manahan, O.S.B.

The Liturgical Press is grateful to Libraria Editrice Vaticana for permission to reprint the English translation of *Liturgiam Authenticam,* © 2001 Libreria Editrice Vaticana, Vatican City.

1   2   3   4   5   6   7   8

Library of Congress Cataloging-in-Publication Data

Jeffery, Peter, 1953–
    Translating tradition : a chant historian reads Liturgiam authenticam / Peter Jeffery ; with an introduction by R. Kevin Seasoltz.
        p. cm.
    "A Pueblo book."
    Summary: "A critique of Liturgiam authenticam, issued by the Roman Catholic Church's Congregation of Divine Worship and the Discipline of the Sacraments (2001)"—Provided by publisher.
    Includes bibliographical references and index.
    ISBN-10: 0-8146-6211-0 (pbk. : alk. paper)
    ISBN-13: 978-0-8146-6211-3 (pbk. : alk. paper)
        1. Catholic Church. Congregatio de Cultu Divino et Disciplina Sacramentorum. Liturgiam authenticam. 2. Liturgical language—English. I. Title.

BX1970.A353J44 2005
264'.02'0014—dc22

                                                    2005008498

Contents

Introduction
  by R. Kevin Seasoltz, O.S.B.   7

CHAPTER ONE
The Latin Liturgical Traditions   9

  Appendix A   30

CHAPTER TWO
The Bible in the Roman Rite   32

  Appendix B   56

CHAPTER THREE
Languages and Cultures   58

CHAPTER FOUR
Human and Angelic Tongues   88

APPENDIX
English translation of *Liturgiam Authenticam*   121

Introduction

It is well known in canonical circles that legislators cannot speak but from within their own cultural context, since they do not live in a vacuum but are influenced by their cultural milieu. Therefore laws almost always reflect the context out of which they are written. In recent years liturgical scholars have wondered about the cultural context of liturgical legislators in the Congregation for Divine Worship and the Discipline of the Sacraments. Concerned about the quality and scholarship of various documents, they wonder where they are coming from.

Cardinal Jorge Medina Estévez, a native Chilean, was the prefect of the Congregation for Divine Worship and the Discipline of the Sacraments from February 1998 until September 2002. Along with Cardinal Joseph Ratzinger, Cardinal Medina was of the opinion that the liturgical reforms unleashed by the Second Vatican Council were going too far. As a matter of fact, that view had deep roots. On October 11, 1972, Cardinal Medina, Cardinal Ratzinger and six other members of the International Theological Commission wrote to Pope Paul VI to express their urgent concern that the unity and purity of the Catholic faith were being severely compromised by inaccurate and theologically suspect translations of liturgical texts from Latin into the vernacular languages. They complained that the Congregation for Divine Worship was unwisely relying on local bishops' conferences to judge the quality of translated texts rather than examining them carefully in Rome. Then twenty-five years later, when Cardinal Medina was appointed prefect of the Congregation for Divine Worship, it was with a clear sense of what he thought had to be done: radically change the structures that had engineered the liturgical reform.

In just less than five years, Cardinal Medina managed to implement sweeping changes in the rules according to which liturgical texts are translated into the vernacular languages, insisting on a much more literal rather than dynamic approach. He also effected radical changes in the structure of the International Commission on English in the Liturgy and prepared the way for the promulgation of the document *Liturgiam Authenticam,* thus giving Rome much more control of the liturgy rather than the bishops' conferences.

In 2004 Peter Jeffery, a brilliant chant historian on the music faculty at Princeton University, wrote four remarkable articles for the liturgical journal *Worship* evaluating at length the content of *Liturgiam Authenticam.* He not only pointed out major inaccuracies in the document but amassed an enormous amount of historical, biblical, liturgical, and cultural scholarship. Dr. Jeffery admits that he is a very conservative and in many ways a traditional Catholic, but his measured and informed articles have been highly praised by liturgical scholars from both the "right" and the "left." Because the articles have lasting value and their content is apt to get lost, Liturgical Press has decided to bring them together in book form. I hope this slim volume will reach a wide readership.

R. Kevin Seasoltz, O.S.B.
Editor, *Worship*

Chapter One

The Latin Liturgical Traditions

Liturgiam Authenticam (hereafter *LA*), issued by the Congregation for Divine Worship and the Discipline of the Sacraments (CDW) on 28 March 2001, lays down new rules (as its subtitle states) "on the use of vernacular languages in the publication of the books of the Roman liturgy."[1] Officially classified as the "Fifth Instruction 'for the Right Implementation of the Constitution on the Sacred Liturgy'," it promises to begin "a new era" in liturgical practice (paragraphs 7, 131). The authors of the statement believe that many of the texts being used "in various localities stand in need of improvement. . . . The omissions or errors which affect certain existing vernacular translations — especially in the case of certain languages — have impeded the progress of the inculturation that actually should have taken place" (6). Instead, *LA* calls for texts that are "marked by sound doctrine, . . . exact in wording, free from all ideological influence, and otherwise endowed with those qualities by which the sacred mysteries of salvation and the indefectible faith of the Church are efficaciously transmitted" (paragraph 3). Though *LA* does not explicitly list for us what "those qualities" are, it is clear from what it does say that the texts we have been using for Catholic worship in English are about to be revised substantially.

---

[1] Official Latin text published in *Notitiae* 416–417 = 37:3-4 (2001) 120–74. I quote, using paragraph numbers, from the English translation published on pp. 123–65 of this book, see below. A Latin-English edition has been published by the United States Conference of Catholic Bishops (Washington, D.C. 2001).

Since significant and widespread change is promised, it is not surprising that *LA* has provoked much comment, both positive and negative, from many people involved with the liturgy. Some grass-roots organizations have praised the document, which they hope will end aspects of North American liturgical practice that they have been critical of. Catholic biblical scholars have been particularly articulate in explaining that the document's prescriptions would weaken, rather than improve, the quality of biblical translations.[2] Liturgical scholars, on the other hand, tend to see it as retrogressive, embodying an inadequate conception of liturgical language. Since the instruction's directives would effectively end the use of gender-inclusive language, some have reacted with hope or fear that that is, in fact, its primary target.

And yet, *LA* does not make a direct argument against inclusive language as such. It affirms that "any prejudice or unjust discrimination on the basis of persons, gender, social condition, race or other criteria . . . has no foundation at all in the texts of the Sacred Liturgy." In spite of this, translators are not to alter "either a biblical text or a liturgical text that has been duly promulgated" (29), even to make the wording more inclusive; it will be the responsibility of homilists and catechists "to transmit [the] right interpretation of the texts," showing that no discrimination is implied or intended. It is almost as if the disappearance of inclusive language would be an unfortunate, unintended after-effect of translation changes that are actually called for by different principles — principles so important that they outweigh whatever arguments there may be for modifying the liturgical texts to express inclusion. A thoughtful and respectful reading of *LA*, therefore, should seek to identify and isolate the core principles that underlie the document's demands and govern its reasoning. Only then, in my view, can we be sure we understand what the document is really saying, and its relationship to other ecclesiastical teaching. It is that sort of reading that I will attempt here.

[2] See, for example, the letter "To the Prelates of the U.S. Conference of Catholic Bishops" from the Executive Board of the Catholic Biblical Association, which in August 2003 was available at http://cba.cua.edu/usccbdoc.cfm (accessed May 2005).

LA begins with two novel (and perhaps conflicting) claims. The first: if Vatican II emphasized the importance of protecting the Eastern rites from being overwhelmed by Western practices and cultural traditions, so the Roman rite is now in need of similar protection; "the same vigilance is required for the safeguarding and the authentic development of the liturgical rites, the ecclesiastical traditions, and the discipline of the Latin Church, and in particular, of the Roman Rite" (4). The use of the phrase "Latin Church" is somewhat curious. The Roman rite, of course, was historically one of several traditions that emerged in Latin-speaking Western Europe, along with the rites of other major centers (Milan, Ravenna, Lyon, Benevento, etc.) and regions (the Gallican rite in what is now France, the Mozarabic rite in Spain, the usages of the continental Irish monasteries). But it is a stretch to imply that these different traditions had enough in common to constitute a liturgical unity which could be characterized as "the discipline of the Latin Church." Even if they did, it is doubtful that "the Latin Church" is a concept many people identify with in this age of vernacular worship. Do the millions of Africans, Asians, North and South Americans, and residents of the Pacific who use the Roman rite today think of themselves as belonging to "the Latin Church"? Even "the Western church" seems an inadequate description for a liturgical tradition that is now observed all over the world.

This brings us to the second claim: it is also something new to see the Roman rite praised as "a precious example and an instrument of true inculturation" (5). Throughout history, advocates of strongly centralized, Rome-based liturgy have tended to argue that Rome was the place where all local expressions of Christianity initially came from — for which reason any problems could be solved simply by re-conforming to whatever Rome was currently doing. Thus a long cast of characters, from the truculent eighth-century author of the *Instructio Ecclesiastici Ordinis*[3] to Dom Prosper

---

[3] Peter Jeffery, "Eastern and Western Elements in the Irish Monastic Prayer of the Hours," *The Divine Office in the Latin Middle Ages: Methodology and Source Studies, Regional Developments, Hagiography, Written in Honor of Professor Ruth Steiner,* ed. Margot E. Fassler and Rebecca A. Baltzer (Oxford University Press 2000) 99–143; see 128–30.

The Latin Liturgical Traditions

Guéranger,[4] have looked to the Roman rite to save us from the heterodox variety and rubrical chaos of the variegated local traditions — if only we would turn, as Charlemagne apocryphally put it, from the polluted stream to the pure source.[5] In calling the Roman rite an "example" of inculturation, therefore, *LA* seems to be taking a positive step, acknowledging modern historical findings that the Roman rite is actually a hybrid. Roman, Irish, Anglo-Saxon, Lombard, Frankish, Visigothic and other Christians all contributed to its development, while pilgrims returning from Jerusalem and Egypt introduced texts and customs from even farther away. Reconsidering the processes by which this happened could be very instructive for us today, as we negotiate issues of inculturation and liturgical renewal. Unfortunately, *LA* does not appear to be advocating that today's inculturation efforts be better informed by history.

Instead, the emphasis seems to be on the Roman rite as an "instrument," rather than an "example," of inculturation. For instance, we are reminded that "the introduction of languages into liturgical use by the Church may actually affect the development of the language itself" (14). But little is said about the reverse possibility, that local languages, or the very act of wrestling with the complex issues encountered in making a translation, might prompt new insights and understandings that could contribute to a more general reshaping of liturgical speech, possibly influencing and benefiting the larger church. For the authors of *LA*, it seems, the Roman rite can inoculate the cultures of the world with Roman Catholic traditions and values, but it has little to learn from the vast array of human experience and creativity that it will encounter in our increasingly interconnected world.

---

[4] "From the haughty dominatrix of the nations that she had been, Rome, through charity, became the mother of the peoples." Prosper Guéranger, *L'Année liturgique* 1: *L'Avent et Noël,* new revised edition (Paris, Tournai; Rome: Desclée 1948) 644.

[5] Joannes Diaconus, *Vita Gregorii* in *Patrologia Latina* [hereafter *PL*] 75:91. See Peter Jeffery, "Rome and Jerusalem: From Oral Tradition to Written Repertory in Two Ancient Liturgical Centers," *Essays on Medieval Music in Honor of David Hughes,* ed. Graeme M. Boone, Isham Library Papers 4 (Cambridge, Mass.: Harvard University Department of Music 1995) 207–47, especially 232–41.

The one-sidedness of the *LA* authors' view becomes especially clear if we look more carefully at their analogy with the Eastern rites. What Vatican II actually taught was that all rites, Eastern and Western, are to "enjoy equal dignity, so that none of them ranks higher than the others."[6] This was a deliberate reversal of more than two centuries of papal teaching that the Roman rite was superior,[7] which in turn had served as the justification for replacing Eastern customs and practices with Western ones. For example, centuries of papal decisions had forbidden Eastern-rite priests to administer the sacrament of confirmation (i.e., what the Orthodox churches call "chrismation"), since in the West this is normally reserved to bishops. Yet Vatican II restored confirmation by priests and other Eastern practices, teaching that "the catholic church wishes that the traditions of each individual church or rite be kept whole and entire."[8] To that end the Council urged that Eastern clergy and laity should be "carefully instructed": "they should have recourse to their age-old traditions."[9] In short, the Council shifted from an ideal of Rome-dominated uniformity to one that the Code of Canons of the Eastern Churches describes as "the patrimony of the universal Church of Christ, which in its diversity [*varietas*] affirms the unity of the catholic faith," for in this patrimony "that tradition shines forth which is from the Apostles through the Fathers."[10]

The fact that the Code of Canons of the Eastern Churches was issued in Latin, rather than an Eastern language, shows how far we still have to go to achieve the ideals of equality of rites and

[6] *Orientalium Ecclesiarum* [= OE] 3, as translated in Norman P. Tanner, et al., eds., *Decrees of the Ecumenical Councils*, 2 vols. (London: Sheed and Ward; Washington, D.C.: Georgetown University Press 1990) 2:901.

[7] George Nedungatt, ed., *A Guide to the Eastern Code: A Commentary on the Code of Canons of the Eastern Churches*, Kanonika 10 (Rome: Pontificio Istituto Orientale 2002) 112–13.

[8] *Orientalium Ecclesiarum* 2, *Decrees* 2:900-01.

[9] *Orientalium Ecclesiarum* 6, *Decrees* 2:902.

[10] Canon 39. This is my own rendition. Though I have in effect resorted to paraphrase by inserting "for in this patrimony" outside the quotation marks, I believe this renders the Latin more exactly than the rather literal translation published in *Code of Canons of the Eastern Churches: Latin-English Edition: Translation prepared under the auspices of the Canon Law Society of America* (Kottayam: Oriental Institute of Religious Studies 1992) 17.

The Latin Liturgical Traditions

diversity affirming unity. But the principles of equality and diversity are what justified the mandate of Vatican II that "all Eastern Christians should know and be certain that they may and should always preserve their own lawful liturgical rites and way of life, and that changes should be made only by reason of their proper and organic development."[11] *LA*'s statements about the need to preserve the Roman rite are similarly worded, which would be fitting if the issue were merely the equality of Eastern and Western rites. The problem emerges when we ask, "What exactly is it that the Roman rite needs to be protected *against?*" There was never, after all, any danger of the Roman rite being overwhelmed by the customs and practices of the East. The unsettling answer is that the authors of *LA* seem to have forgotten the principle underlying the mandate to preserve the Eastern rites — the principle that diversity in equality affirms a more profound unity. Instead, they see the preservation of tradition as a way to resist and limit diversity: "The work of inculturation, of which the translation into vernacular languages is a part, is not therefore to be considered an avenue for the creation of new varieties or families of rites; on the contrary, it should be recognized that any adaptations introduced out of cultural or pastoral necessity thereby became part of the Roman Rite, and are to be inserted into it in a harmonious way" (*LA* 5). By separating the Vatican II directive to preserve traditional rites from the principle it is based on, they have introduced at least an apparent contradiction. For it is one thing to say that a person of Slavonic or Coptic or Syriac heritage should not be hindered in practicing his or her traditional indigenous expression of Christianity. It is quite another to say that a person of non-European heritage should be held to strict limits in developing his or her own indigenous expression of Christianity. Even if these contrary values are somehow both correct, neither can be proven by mere appeal to the other. If we appeal, instead, to the Roman liturgical tradition, what we discover is not a simple solution to the dilemma, but a two-millennia-long debate, involving even its most authoritative spokesmen.

For example, Pope Leo the Great (reigned 440–61) told the bishops of Sicily to "[take] the law of all observance from [the same place]

---

[11] *Orientalium Ecclesiarum* 6, *Decrees* 2:902.

where you accepted consecration to [episcopal] rank. Let the See of the blessed Apostle Peter, which for you is the mother of priestly dignity, also be the teacher of ecclesiastical procedure. . . . In fact the Spirit of wisdom and knowledge instructed the apostles and teachers of the Church, so that in Christian observance nothing may be inordinate, nothing permitted to be confused. The reasons for celebrations are to be understood, and a reasonable discrimination to be observed in all that our Fathers and predecessors have instituted. This is because we are not 'one flock and one shepherd' unless, as the Apostle teaches, 'we all say the same thing: and we all are perfected in the same mind [sensu] and in the same opinion [sententia]'."[12]

On the other hand Pope Gregory the Great (590–604) taught that "Where there is one faith, a diversity of usage does no harm to holy Church."[13] In this spirit he advised his own missionaries: "It is my wish that if you have found any customs in the Roman or the Gaulish church or any other church which may be more pleasing to almighty God, you should make a careful selection of them and sedulously teach . . . what you have been able to gather from other churches. For things are not to be loved for the sake of a place, but places are to be loved for the sake of their good things. Therefore choose from every individual Church whatever things are devout, religious, and right."[14]

For both popes — the only two who are traditionally surnamed "the Great" — unity was a value that could not be compromised. Yet Leo considered it essential to unity that "we all say the same thing," which indeed had to be the apostolic and Roman thing; Gregory thought a unity of faith could co-exist with diversity of usage. The two great popes were not necessarily contradicting each other, of course. Since Leo was writing to suffragan bishops in southern Italy who had been ordained in Rome, we might say in more modern terms that his role as primate of Italy was a factor

[12] *Epistolae* 16.address, and 16.2, in *PL* 54:696, 698, quoting John 10:17 and 1 Corinthians 1:10.
[13] Letter to Leander of Seville in *Registrum Epistularum* 1.41, ed. Dag Norberg in *Corpus Christianorum Series Latina* [= *CCL*] 140 (1982) 48.
[14] Bede, *Historia Ecclesiastica Gentis Anglorum* 1.27, interrogatio 2. Bertram Colgrave and R.A.B. Mynors, eds., *Bede's Ecclesiastical History of the English People*, corrected reprint (Oxford: Clarendon Press 1991) 80–83.

in this case. Gregory, on the other hand, was writing to a bishop in Spain, which had its own primatial see at Toledo, and followed what would become the Mozarabic rite. In any case there were limits even to Gregory's tolerance for diversity: he was one of the popes who forbade (Western) priests to administer confirmation.[15]

So what were Gregory's criteria for managing diversity, to keep it from injuring unity? First of all, Gregory allowed the possibility of multiple interpretations, so that even people who did the same thing could understand it differently. "Now since we immerse three times, we signify the sacraments of the three-day burial; so that, when the infant is lifted out of the waters a third time, the resurrection after a three-day period is expressed. But if perhaps anyone may think it is also in honor of the supreme Trinity, neither is there anything against immersing the person to be baptized in the waters once. For while there is one substance in three subsistences, it cannot possibly be forbidden to immerse the infant in baptism either three times or once, when the trinity of persons can be designated in three immersions, and the singularity of divinity in one." Since some interpretations could lead to misunderstandings, however, Gregory was willing to advise *against* the adoption of Roman practice, when doing so could lead to pastoral problems. "But since up to now the infant has been immersed three times by the heretics, I do not advise it to be done among you, lest while they count the immersions they divide the divinity, and while they do what they have been doing, they boast of having gotten the better of our practice."[16]

Both popes, then, applied the principles of unity and right interpretation according to the situation they were dealing with at the time. Neither can be taken in isolation from the other and touted as expressing the "real" Roman tradition; respect for the full Roman tradition requires us to hold both of them in tension. Leo's concern

---

[15] Pope Innocent I was already taking this position in 416; see Robert Cabié, ed., *La lettre du pape Innocent Ier à Décentius de Gubbio (19 mars 416): Texte critique, traduction et commentaire*, Bibliothèque de la Revue d'histoire ecclésiastique 58 (Louvain: Publications Universitaires 1973) 22–25, 44–48. Gregory forbade priests to administer confirmation in a letter to a bishop in Sardinia, but then permitted it in situations where there was no bishop. *Registrum Epistularum* 4.9 and 4.26, ed. D. Norberg in *CCL* 140:226, 246.

[16] *Registrum Epistularum* 1.43, in *CCL* 140 (1982) 48.

for apostolicity and Gregory's for pastoral impact are both important values; the trick is knowing how to balance them in particular
situations. The problem, then, for those who actually shape liturgical practice — translators, editors, celebrants — will be: How do
we determine if something is consistent with the Roman tradition
or not? If we are not thinking about preserving the Roman rite as
something frozen in time — if, that is, we are open to "harmonious" *(LA)*, "proper and organic development" *(OE)* — how are
we to judge the legitimacy of any specific proposal or change?

Some may think the answer is obvious: all we need to do is forward all questions to Rome for decision. But the most compelling
refutation of this view is *LA* itself, for the people who wrote it are
seriously misinformed about the historical development of the tradition they call on us to preserve. As a historian of liturgical chant,
almost every day I read and sing texts from every period in the
history of the Roman rite — and I find *LA*'s vision of the Roman
tradition impossible to reconcile with what the primary sources
reveal. I agree that the historical integrity of the Roman rite should
be preserved, and my personal tastes (which I rarely indulge) are
as conservative as one can get without rejecting Vatican II. Yet I
cannot imagine how *LA*'s recommendations could possibly be
carried out without causing a massive rupture with the Roman
liturgical tradition as it has historically been.

Being a historian, of course, I cannot speak with authority on
theological or juridical issues — but surely no one would argue
that theological or juridical decisions can be uninformed by sound
historical knowledge. Since *LA* is full of misstatements about the
Roman liturgical tradition, those who wrote and approved it are
simply in no position to judge whether a practice or text is Roman
or not, and as a faithful Catholic it is my religious duty under
Canon 212 Section 3 to respectfully point out the problems.

Of course there are many questions that are properly decided at
the Vatican level, and the definition of the Roman rite is doubtless
one of them. But it goes without saying that such decisions cannot
be made on the basis of the arbitrary or individual preferences of
church officials. They must, instead, be grounded in principles that
can be identified, defined, and explained to the church at large. To
read a document like *LA* with the respect and seriousness that is
called for, then, requires that we ask, "What are the core principles

that govern its logic and reasoning? What values is it seeking to protect, and against whom or what perceived danger?" We have already seen that *LA* invokes the Vatican II demand to preserve the Eastern rites without acknowledging the historical situation or the underlying principle that gave rise to it. What, then, are the real principles that fostered the statements, prescriptions and proscriptions of *LA*?

THE TRADITION OF THE LATIN CHURCH?

"The Creed is to be translated according to the precise wording that the tradition of the Latin Church has bestowed upon it, including the use of the first person singular" (65). Thus *LA* would require "I believe," the literal translation of "Credo," in place of the "We believe" (Latin "Credimus") that we Americans have been saying. The appeal to the "tradition of the Latin Church" is bolstered with a quotation from St Thomas Aquinas, one of only two sources written before 1947 that *LA* cites.[17] The quotation says that the Creed is "handed down . . . as coming from the person of the whole Church, united by means of the Faith" (II-II q. 1, art. 9, ad 3). Does this really prove that saying "We believe" violates "the tradition of the Latin Church"?

LA seems to be saying that, not only the Roman rite, but the broader Latin church as a whole shares a uniform tradition in favor of "I believe," as if "We believe" were essentially an Eastern tradition. But this is simply untrue. The original texts of the so-called "Nicene Creed," as published by the early ecumenical councils, began "We believe," as reported in numerous Latin and Greek sources.[18] The plural "we" form was cited by Pope Leo the Great,[19] and in early Roman collections of canon law, some of which even begin with the words, "The faith of the Romans," or "Here begins the faith of the Catholic Roman Church: We believe in

---

[17] The other is the Council of Trent. Apart from the 1947 encyclical *Mediator Dei* of Pope Pius XII, all other sources cited in *LA* date from 1964 or later — that is, from the Vatican II era.

[18] See, for example, A. E. Burn, ed., *Facsimiles of the Creeds from Early Manuscripts*, Henry Bradshaw Society 36 (London: Harrison and Sons 1909) 13–17, plates XI–XIV. Tanner, *Decrees* 1:5, 24, 64.

[19] *Epistola* 165.3, ed. in *PL* 54:1159, cf. 84:732.

Translating Tradition

one God. . . ."[20] The Mozarabic rite of Spain, the best-documented Latin liturgical tradition after the Roman, has always said "We believe," both before and after Vatican II.[21] Even in the Roman Mass there was a minority tradition that used "Credimus" instead of "Credo." Melodies with this form of the text are preserved in manuscripts of the eleventh and twelfth centuries; one of them is even in the currently authorized chant books (with the text regularized to "Credo").[22] The Eastern churches, too, use both forms. The Coptic, Ethiopian, Chaldean and Armenian rites stay closer to the conciliar originals with "We believe," but the ancient Greek liturgies of Byzantium, Jerusalem, and Egypt use "I believe." In the West Syrian rite, at one time, the priest said "We" while the people said "I."[23]

Even the quote from St Thomas is not, in its original context, an argument against "Credimus" as such. Thomas was responding to a hypothetical proposition that there should not be a Creed at all, on the grounds that those in the congregation who lack "living faith" should not be reciting "I believe in God." His reply that the Creed is recited "from the person of the whole church" means that "Hence the confession of faith is expressed . . . in a manner that is in keeping with living faith, so that even if some of the faithful lack living faith, they should endeavor to acquire it" (II-II q. 1 art. 9, ad 3). We cannot be sure from this that St Thomas would have

[20] PL 56:216 no. CXXIV; cf. PL 56:583, 585; ed. V. Bulhart in CCL 9 (1957) 129 and CCL 69 (1967) 267, 271, 275.

[21] Missale Hispano-Mozarabicum ([Toledo:] Conferencia Episcopal Española, Arzobispado de Toledo 1991) 75. For the medieval Mozarabic rite see PL 85: 117, 139, 486, 557. See also Vincent A. Lenti, "Liturgical Reform and the Ambrosian and Mozarabic Rites," Worship 68 (1994) 417–26, esp 423.

[22] Credo VI, which received ecclesiastical approval in 1913 and has been included in all editions of the Graduale Romanum since then. On the medieval sources see David Hiley, Western Plainchant: A Handbook (Oxford: Clarendon Press 1993) 169–70. For other Credimus texts with melodies see Tadeusz Miazga, Die Melodien des einstimmigen Credo der römisch-katholischen lateinischen Kirche: Eine Untersuchung der Melodien in den handschriftlich Überlieferung mit besonderer Berücksichtigung der polnischen Handschriften (Graz: Akademische Druck 1976) 133–45, esp. pp. 18 and 136.

[23] In F. E. Brightman, Liturgies Eastern and Western 1: Eastern Liturgies (Oxford: Clarendon Press 1896) see pp. 162 (Coptic), 226 (Ethiopian), 270 (Chaldean), 426 (Armenian); 321 and 383 (Byzantine), 42 (Jerusalem), 124 (Egypt); 82 (West Syrian).

The Latin Liturgical Traditions

opposed the "Credimus" opening had he been aware of it. Since he defined "living faith" as "the faith to be found in all those who are of the Church not only outwardly but by merit," it is possible he would have seen value in "Credimus."

In fact, a few paragraphs later Thomas demonstrates an attitude towards creedal variation that is significantly more open than *LA*. He himself preferred the reading *Et unam sanctam* . . ., "And one holy catholic and apostolic Church," over *Et in unam sanctam* . . ., "And *in* one holy catholic and apostolic Church."[24] In his opinion, the word "in" implied that one has faith in the church in the same way one has faith in God. Thomas seems not to have realized that the "in" was part of the original conciliar text, both Latin and Greek, and that his preferred reading, without the "in," was an innovation. What is significant for our purposes, however, is that both readings seem to have been in liturgical use in Thomas's day, and that he accepted this state of affairs. Even though he thought one variant superior to the other, Thomas did not demand that the inferior form be banned or forbidden. Instead he reinterpreted it. He was willing to accept "and *in* one holy catholic and apostolic Church" if it were interpreted to mean "I believe in the Holy Spirit sanctifying the Church" (II-II q. 1 a. 9, ad 5). St Thomas was no Latitudinarian — only a few pages later we find him justifying the torture of heretics and war against infidels. In accepting multiple alternatives he was simply following the common practice of scholastic theology, encapsulated in the maxim *diversi, sed non adversi* — church tradition may exhibit variations, but these variations are not opposed to each other. The reconciliation of apparently contradictory traditions was an essential part of the training of scholastic theologians, which they learned by writing commentaries on the *Sentences* of Peter Lombard. Thus, while we cannot know exactly what St Thomas would have said about "Credimus" as an alternative to "Credo," his overall approach was fundamentally different from the position in support of which *LA* cites him:

[24] The reading Thomas preferred, without "in," has been the reading of the Roman Missal since at least the first printed edition of 1474. However, the English translation we have been using says we believe "in one holy Catholic apostolic Church," the inferior reading in Thomas's view. Is this a case where the "stability" of the translation should be "maintained," as directed in *LA* Paragraph 74?

Translating Tradition

He did not believe that all Western Christians must recite the Creed with exactly the same wording.

The wording St Thomas preferred, without the "in," eventually became the standard text of the Roman Missal, at the latest by the time of its first printed edition in 1474. In this form it was cited by the Council of Trent and Vatican I,[25] while the Eastern churches (and also our current English translation!) continued to use the original wording, including the "in." One might argue, of course, that the "Credo" opening, like the omission of "in," has now become the standard wording of the Roman rite (though not of the Latin liturgical tradition as a whole), so that the CDW no longer has the authority to permit a return to the original wording, "Credimus." But this would be a difficult position to defend, given the liturgical renewal that began with Vatican II. We now use a Missal in which many disused medieval prayers have been revived, as well as an Eastern eucharistic prayer (#4) and other texts that have no precedent at all in Latin liturgical traditions.[26] In any case it is undercut by the fact that the CDW has already authorized a change in another ancient creed.

This change was made in the wording of the so-called Apostles' Creed. Since it emerged in the context of the Roman baptismal rite and has no exact Eastern counterpart, the Apostles' Creed is un-arguably a core text of the Roman liturgical tradition. For centuries it has begun *Credo in Deum*, "I believe in God," a reading preserved even after Vatican II in the Missal of Paul VI, the Rite of Christian Initiation, and the Catechism of the Catholic Church.[27] Yet in the

---

[25] Tanner, *Decrees* 2:662, 802.

[26] For example the acclamation after the consecration, which has no antecedents in the Latin rites, was introduced in imitation of the West Syrian rite. Catholic writers on liturgy tend not to mention that the first western-derived liturgy to do this was that of the Church of South India (a union of Protestant denominations) in 1950; see Bernard Wigan, ed., *The Liturgy in English* (London: Oxford University Press 1962) 215.

[27] "Credo in Deum" will be found in the baptismal rite in every edition of the pre-Conciliar *Rituale Romanum,* and still in *Ordo Initiationis Christianae Adultorum,* Editio Typica (Typis Polyglottis Vaticanis 1972) 76. The English translation of the *Catechism of the Catholic Church* says "We begin our profession of faith by saying: 'I believe' or 'we believe" (paragraph 26); paragraphs 199–200 clearly distinguish the Apostles' Creed ("I believe in God") from the Niceno-Constantinopolitan Creed ("I believe in one God"). "Credo in unum Deum" occurs in paragraph 19

new *Missale Romanum* of 2002 we find it beginning *Credo in unum Deum*, "I believe in *one* God" — a variant with far less historical precedent in the Apostles' Creed than "Credimus" has in the Nicene Creed.[28] Unless the CDW identifies this as an error and issues a correction, then, translators will find themselves in an absurd position: We may *not* use the plural "We believe" opening, despite all its conciliar and liturgical precedent in East and West, because *LA* asserts that doing so would violate the Latin liturgical tradition. But we *must* translate the Apostles' Creed with "I believe in one God" because . . . well, because the authorities have seen fit to alter the ancient text, in opposition to Roman tradition.

Unfortunately this case is no fluke. Inaccuracies, misrepresentations and contradictions so abound in *LA* that anyone who tried to obey it religiously would find himself hopelessly mired in absurdities, demonstrating fidelity to Roman tradition by doing and saying things that are neither Roman nor traditional. I only have space to point out the most obvious examples.

RESPECT FOR THE TEXT?

LA demands very exact, closely literal translations, reproducing as much as possible the semantic fields, the fine nuances, the varied vocabulary, even the capitalization (33)[29] of the Latin originals.

---

of the Ordo Missae in *Missale Romanum,* Editio Typica Tertia (Typis Vaticanis 2002) 513.

[28] Among other things, Pope Leo cited the Apostles' Creed without "unum" in his *Tomus ad Flavianum,* see Tanner, *Decrees* 1:77, *PL* 54:757. For this he was attacked by the Eutychianists, and defended by Vigilius of Thapsus: *PL* 62:119 (see also 50:475, 55:185). About the year 400, Rufinus stated that the Roman church preserved the ancient tradition of having the creed recited publicly at baptismal liturgies without the word "unum," because at Rome there was no need to be concerned about heresy (*Expositio Symboli* 3, CCL 20 [1961] 135–36). This makes it difficult to argue that including "unum" in the Apostles' Creed represents the Roman tradition better than keeping it out. For more on the history of the text see: Wolfram Kinzig, Christoph Markschies, Markus Vinzent, *Tauffragen und Bekenntnis: Studien zur sogenannten 'Traditio Apostolica' zu den 'Interrogationes de fide' und zum 'Römischen Glaubensbekenntnis',* Arbeiten zur Kirchengeschichte 74 (Berlin: Walter de Gruyter 1999). Heinrich Denzinger, *Enchiridion Symbolorum Definitionum et Declarationum de Rebus Fidei et Morum,* 37th ed., ed. and trans. Peter Hünermann (Freiburg im Breisgau: Herder 1991) 21–48, 62–64, 72–76, 83–85.

[29] This attempt to standardize capitalization seems unprecedented to me. Though I am unaware of a published study on the subject, I have personally

Personally, I am inclined to be sympathetic to this position. There is the well-known case of the Christmas collect that speaks in Latin of what God has done wonderfully and more wonderfully, but in English of what we do and then do more of.[30] Again, I would much prefer to sing "Save us, O Savior of the world, who delivered us by your cross and resurrection!" than the relentlessly monosyllabic "Lord, by your cross and resurrection you have set us free; you are the savior of the world," which always reminds me of reading *Fun with Dick and Jane* in first grade. But I do not believe these infelicities stem from the translators' lack of faith, or what *LA* calls "a psychologizing tendency" (54). I think they originated in attempts to evade the relative clause, in the belief that it constitutes an "expression . . . which is confusing or ambiguous when heard" (44, cf. 27). Thus the real issue is how to translate texts that are supposed to be apprehended orally, so that individual worshipers will not need to look at a written text during the celebration itself.

Typical of *LA*'s ideal is its statement that "Whenever the biblical or liturgical text preserves words taken from other ancient languages . . . consideration should be given to preserving the same words in the new vernacular translation, at least as one option among others. Indeed, a careful respect for the original text will sometimes require that this be done" (23). This prescription, which refers to words that the Latin texts quote in Greek, Hebrew, and Aramaic, is more accepting of variation than the insistence on "Credo" over "Credimus." But one is left wondering what are the times or circumstances in which preservation of the ancient language will be "required." When we look at the histories of specific words, however, we find that the Roman rite and other liturgical traditions have never taken a uniform approach to the question of

---

examined many printed editions of the Roman Missal from the fifteenth century to the present. I found wide variation in capitalization practice, both over time and from one publisher to another. In general, the historical trend was to capitalize more and more words, peaking with the second Missal of Leo XIII (1900), then lurching to the other extreme of minimal capitalization in 1962. Discussions within the Catholic Academy of Liturgy have brought to my attention the fact that there are also significant capitalization differences between the original text of the new *Instructio Generalis Missalis Romani* (2000) and the text published in the 2002 *Missale Romanum*.

[30] Richard Toporoski, "The Language of Worship," *Communio* 4 (1977) 226–60, see p. 240; or the abridged recension in *Worship* 52 (1978) 489–508, see 499.

leaving such terms in the original language — a demand that we do so now cannot be justified as preserving Roman tradition.

The Kyrie. A number of historical elements combined to form the Kyrie eleison of the Roman Mass. Nowadays the phrase "Lord, have mercy" is understood as an expression of contrition; the reforms after Vatican II have reinforced this interpretation. But originally it had a wider range of applicability: passages like Matthew 20:30-31 show that the phrase could also be used in contexts of petition. Thus medieval litanies, both Eastern and Western, often had "Kyrie eleison" serving as the congregational response or refrain.[31] The Kyrie of the Mass seems to be the remnant of such a litany, sung upon entering the church or the altar area, after the processional introit. But "Kyrie eleison" has had many other uses in the various liturgical traditions: as preparation for collects,[32] at dismissals and the prayers of the faithful, while venerating relics of the cross, for example. The Western rites of Rome and Milan, and the Coptic and West Syrian rites in the East, have continued to say "Kyrie eleison" in the original Greek. But it has traditionally been translated in the Byzantine-Slavonic rite *(Gospodi pomiluĭ)* and the Armenian rite *(Dēr voghormya)*. Almost the only surviving excerpt of the liturgy of the Arian Goths is their translation of "Kyrie eleison" *(Sihora armen).*[33] In the Mozarabic rite, at the Good Friday veneration of the Cross, the word *Indulgentia!* (Latin for "forgiveness") was repeated a hundred or more times as a counterpart to the repeated "Kyrie eleison" of the Greek liturgies for the cross.[34]

Even in the Roman rite, however, there is some precedent for translating the Kyrie. It is translated in the Slavonic version of the Roman Missal, used in Croatia since the Middle Ages (sometimes

---

[31] For an introduction to the subject see Peter Jeffery, "Litany," *Dictionary of the Middle Ages* 7 (New York: Scribner 1986) 588–94.

[32] Robert Taft, *Beyond East and West: Problems in Liturgical Understanding* (Washington, D.C.: Pastoral Press 1984) 154–56.

[33] *PL* 33:1162.

[34] Marius Férotin, ed., *Le Liber mozarabicus sacramentorum et les manuscrits mozarabes,* Monumenta Ecclesiae Liturgica 6 (Paris: Firmin-Didot 1912; repr. Farnborough: Gregg 1969) XXXVII, 734–35. Mother Mary and Kallistos Ware, *The Festal Menaion* (London: Faber and Faber 1969, repr. 1984) 153–55.

called the "Glagolitic rite").[35] As Egeria attests, Latin litanies often used *Domine miserere* and similar expressions as the response, interchangeably with "Kyrie eleison" in Greek.[36] In fact the *Deprecatio* ascribed to Pope Gelasius, thought to be a direct ancestor of the Kyrie in the Roman Mass, has the Greek response "Kyrie eleison" in one manuscript, but Latin *Domine exaudi et miserere* ("Lord, hear and have mercy") in two others, and *Domine miserere et miserere* ("Lord, have mercy and have mercy") in a fourth MS.[37] Some of the medieval Kyrie tropes (which it is better to call *prosulae*) put the words "Domine miserere" and other Latin renditions right into the Mass Kyrie itself. The example in Appendix A (p. 30) is unusual in that it seems to have begun as a litany for vespers in Holy Week, and only subsequently been remodeled into a Kyrie prosula. But it demonstrates that singing translations of "Kyrie eleison" in the Roman Mass was not considered disrespectful of the original text.[38]

Our example also highlights the problematic relationship of the Kyrie prosulae to the current Roman Missal. Contrary to much popular belief the tropes were not banned by the Council of Trent, they were simply not included in the 1570 Missal — probably because they had always been specific to local diocesan propers, and in any case had been dying out for several centuries; there is no reason to think they were ever regarded as theologically suspect. Once the Missal of Trent was adopted, however, the tropes were automatically excluded by directives that nothing could be added to the approved text. After Vatican II, though, the General Instruction

[35] Eve-Marie Schmidt-Deeg, ed., *Das New Yorker Missale: Eine kroato-glagolitische Handschrift des frühen 15. Jahrhunderts,* Sagners Slavistische Sammlung 22 (Munich: Otto Sagner 1994) 350, col. d, line 26.

[36] *Itinerarium* 24.5, see Égérie, *Journal de Voyage (Itinéraire),* ed. Pierre Maraval, rev. ed., Sources Chrétiennes 296 (Paris: Éditions du Cerf 2002) 240–41.

[37] B. Capelle, "Le *Kyrie* de la Messe et le pape Gélase," *Revue Bénédictine* 46 (1934) 126–44. Paul De Clerck, *La "prière universelle" dans les liturgies latines anciennes: témoignages patristiques et textes liturgiques,* Liturgiewissenschaftliche Quellen und Forschungen 62 (Münster: Aschendorff 1977) 166–87.

[38] The largest published collection of Kyrie tropes is still Clemens Blume and Guido M. Dreves, eds., *Analecta Hymnica Medii Aevi 47: Tropi Graduales: Tropen des Missale im Mittelalter* (Leipzig: O. R. Reisland 1905) 45–216. For texts that include Latin translations of the liturgical Greek text, see nos. 1 p. 45, 127 p. 184, 130 p. 187, 131 p. 188, 132 p. 189, 160 p. 213.

of the Roman Missal explicitly permitted Kyrie tropes again[39] —
the only point where it mentioned tropes of any kind. However the
new third edition of the General Instruction apparently introduces
a new restriction, saying "When the Kyrie is sung as part of the
penitential rite, a 'trope' is placed before each acclamation."[40] This
refers to the text *Qui missus es sanare*, "You were sent to heal the
contrite . . .," which resembles some medieval tropes but was actually composed anew for the 1970 edition of the Missal, as a
model for improvisation by the priest.[41] A literal reading of the
current liturgical norm, then, would be that "tropes" may be said
only when using that form of the penitential rite that incorporates
"Qui missus es" with the response "Kyrie eleison" — I find no
mention of leaving the wording to the priest. Since this text —
indeed the whole penitential rite as we know it — is less than forty
years old, it should not be identified with the ancient Kyrie and its
prosulae, but only as derived from or inspired by them. But if that
is the case, once again the result is absurdity. If we use the 1970
penitential rite, how can we be "required" to say it in an ancient
language? If we follow the more traditional option, reciting the
Confiteor and then singing the Kyrie afterward, why should we not
translate it as the Slavonic Missal and some Latin tropes have done?

The Trisagion. The trisagion of Good Friday is another text for
which "respect for the original text" will "sometimes require"
retention of Greek (23). But the liturgical traditions provide even
less support for this position than they do for the Kyrie. The trisagion
is translated in every rite that uses it in the Ordinary of the Mass
(Syrian, Slavonic, Armenian, Ethiopian), except the Coptic, which
preserved many of its sung Ordinary texts in Greek, even after the
prayers of the priest shifted to Coptic. In Arabic texts of the Coptic
rite, however, the trisagion is translated.[42] The pre-Conciliar

---

[39] "a short verse (trope) may be interpolated" (paragraph 30).

[40] "Quando *Kyrie* cantatur ut pars actus paenitentialis, singulis acclamationibus
'tropus' praeponitur." *Institutio Generalis* (2002) paragraph 52.

[41] "The actual wording is left to the celebrating priest," according to Josef A.
Jungmann, *The Mass: an historical, theological, and pastoral survey*, trans. Julian
Fernandes, ed. Mary Ellen Evans (Collegeville, Minn.: The Liturgical Press 1976)
168.

[42] *Pievshologion nte ti-ekklésia nalexandriné* (Rome: Tipografia S. Pio X 1971) 226.

Roman rite, too, translated the trisagion into Latin wherever it was used, such as the *preces feriales* at Prime, and the Procession for Any Tribulation.[43] The Good Friday trisagion was sung by two choirs alternating in Greek and Latin (or Greek and Slavonic), as it still is in the present Latin missal. The reason for maintaining Greek alongside the Latin, however, was something a lot more complex than "respect for the text."

The singing of the trisagion on Good Friday did not originate in Rome; it was one of those "imaginative and dramatic elements . . . [that] were introduced into the Roman liturgy by the Gallo-Frankish reformers" when the Roman rite was imported into northern Europe.[44] It is a specific example of a more widespread practice of singing texts in Greek — not necessarily the trisagion — at ceremonies honoring the Holy Cross, in imitation of the liturgies celebrated at Jerusalem on Good Friday, September 14, and mid-Lent. Thus the Ethiopian rite, like the Coptic, sings "Remember me when you come into your kingdom" in Greek.[45] This served at Jerusalem as the refrain to the beatitudes, sung on Good Friday at the station in the Garden of Olives.[46] Troparia incorporating this refrain are still sung with the Beatitudes in the Byzantine rite.[47] In Spain the

[43] *Rituale Romanum,* Tit. IX, Cap. 12. For a medieval custom of reciting it after the elevation at Mass, as a prayer for the success of the Crusades, see Amnon Linder, *Raising Arms: Liturgy in the Struggle to Liberate Jerusalem in the Late Middle Ages,* Cultural Encounter in Late Antiquity and the Middle Ages 2 (Turnhout: Brepols 2003) 260.

[44] "The Franco-German clergy did not look upon their new liturgy as a treasure which was not to be meddled with and which they merely had to pass on. . . . During the eighth and ninth centuries, the Franks boldly developed the liturgy they had inherited, exercising at the same time a high degree of creative ability." Theodor Klauser, *A Short History of the Western Liturgy: An account and some reflections,* 2nd ed., trans. John Halliburton (Oxford University Press 1979) 81, 78.

[45] Kay Kaufman Shelemay and Peter Jeffery, *Ethiopian Christian Liturgical Chant: An Anthology* 2: *Performance Practice, The Liturgical Portions,* Recent Researches in the Oral Traditions of Music 2 (Madison, Wisconsin: A–R Editions 1994) 54–55, 96–97.

[46] Athanasios Papadopoulos-Keramefs, Ἀνάλεκτα Ἱεροσολυμιτικῆς Σταχυολογίας 2 (St Petersburg: Kirschbaum 1894; repr. Brussels: Culture et Civilisation 1963) 133–36.

[47] Mother Mary and Kallistos Ware, *The Lenten Triodion* (London: Faber and Faber 1978, repr. 1984) 589–90.

Mozarabic rite also sang "Remember me" on Good Friday, but in Latin and as the refrain to Psalm 50 [51].[48]

The original Roman way of paralleling Jerusalem practice was to celebrate the stational liturgy at the church called "Holy Cross in Jerusalem," where the local relics of the passion were and still are kept. Since this Roman location could not be duplicated outside the city, the Frankish adaptors of the Roman rite found another way of recalling the city where Jesus died, by introducing the trisagion. Readily recognized in the West as emblematic of the Christian East, the trisagion had also had long use in the Gallican and Mozarabic Ordinary of the Mass, where it was sung in both Latin and Greek. Its use on Good Friday, therefore, not only recalled the True Cross in Jerusalem, but the indigenous Gallican rite that Charlemagne and his father had suppressed in favor of the Roman.

Thus the history of the trisagion enfolds many stories relevant to the issues *LA* addresses: the preservation of rites and traditions, the positions of Jerusalem and Rome as centers to be emulated, and relationships among liturgical languages. An involved argument could be made that singing the Good Friday trisagion in Greek (in alternation with Latin or another language) serves as a reminder of the Holy Places where the historical Jesus suffered, of the ancient services for venerating the True Cross, and of Christendom's primeval liturgical tradition centered in its holy city. Referencing such things in modern worship could be justified, on *LA*'s terms, as preserving an element of the historic Roman rite, and emphasizing some of the non-Roman elements that make the Roman rite "a precious example . . . of true inculturation" (5). These values would be served even more fully by the use of the traditional Gregorian chant melody, which preserves musical relationships to Eastern melodies that may owe something to the tune sung in Jerusalem itself.[49] However, *LA* does not actually make these arguments, but speaks only of "respect for the text." In fact the histories of the

---

[48] Marius Férotin, ed., *Le Liber Ordinum en usage dans l'église wisigothique et mozarabe d'Espagne du cinquième au onzième siècle,* Monumenta Ecclesiae Liturgica 5 (Paris: Firmin-Didot 1904; repr. Farnborough: Gregg 1969) 201–2.

[49] Kenneth Levy, "The Trisagion in Byzantium and the West," *International Musicological Society: Report of the Eleventh Congress, Copenhagen 1972* (Copenhagen: Wilhelm Hansen n.d.) 2:761-65.

Kyrie and the trisagion show that the liturgical traditions, including the Roman rite, offered more than one answer to the question of whether to translate from Greek. When we turn to the Semitic words used within Christian worship, we find even greater diversity.

Semitic words. Contrary to ancient legend, the Greek Septuagint translation of the Old Testament was not produced in a single effort; the various books were translated independently, sometimes more than once, within the Alexandrian Jewish community over the last centuries before the Common Era. It would not be surprising, then, if translation practices differed from one book to another, and in fact they do. The word "Halleluia," which occurs mainly in the Psalter, is generally transliterated from the original Hebrew, dropping only the initial H (due to the peculiarities of Greek spelling). The word "Amen," however, is translated in most books of the Septuagint *(genoito!),* except in Chronicles and Nehemiah, where it is transliterated *(amen!).* The Greek New Testament, on the other hand, repeatedly uses the transliterated Amen, either because it was remembered as something Jesus said, or perhaps because it had achieved liturgical use among Hellenistic Jews, which Christians continued. In modern worship, then, should we say "Amen" or "So be it" (or "genoito")? The Greek Bible offers mixed, inconsistent answers, but things get worse when we turn to the Latin Bible. The Latin Vulgate keeps Amen in Hebrew almost throughout, except in the most liturgical part, the Psalms, where it translates it *(fiat!).* In this it follows the practice of the Old Roman Psalter, the most substantial witness to the earliest Roman liturgical tradition.[50]

Should we translate "Amen," then? Even the Roman rite answers both yes and no. Nor is it consistent about other Semitic words. Septuagint, Vulgate, and Old Roman psalters all translate "Hosanna" at Psalm 117[118]:25, but the New Testament maintains it in Hebrew — indeed unintelligibly so.[51] The Septuagint of

---

[50] Robert Weber, ed., *Le Psautier romain et les autres anciens psautiers latins: Édition critique,* Collectanea Biblica Latina 10 (Rome: Abbaye Saint-Jérome, Vatican City: Libreria Vaticana 1953) 90, 168, 223, 269.

[51] See the remarks in W. F. Albright and C. S. Mann, *Matthew,* The Anchor Bible (Garden City: Doubleday 1971) 252. On the other hand, in Revelation 7:10 it is paraphrased by the Greek word *soteria* (salvation).

Isaiah 6:3 keeps the Hebrew transliteration "Sabaoth," as does the Sanctus in every edition of the *Missale Romanum* — but the Vulgate translates it *(exercituum)*. The rite of baptism, both before and after Vatican II, maintains the Aramaic word "Ephpheta" (from Mark 7:34), but also translates it, as indeed the Gospel itself does: *quod est Adaperire* ("that is, 'Be opened!'").

Do the texts of the Roman rite teach that Greek and Semitic words are preferably kept in the original language? The answer is a resounding "sometimes." There are precedents for translating and precedents for not translating, so that factors besides "respect for the text" must be taken into account. Even on words as prominent as Amen, Hosanna, and Sabaoth, the Roman Mass disagrees with the Latin Vulgate. *Diversi, sed non adversi.* In fact the relationship between bible and liturgy in the history of the Roman rite is very complex, and the recent liturgical reforms have added new kinds of complexity. This will be the subject of the next chapter.

Appendix A
Kyrieleyson. Domine miserere.
Kyrie. Qui passurus aduenisti propter nos.
Kyrie. Qui expansis manibus in cruce traxisti omnia ad te secula.
Kyrie. Qui prophetice promisisti ero mors tua o mors.

Christe. Christus dominus factus est obediens usque ad mortem
    mortem autem crucis.
Christe. Vita in ligno moritur infernus et morsus dispoliatur.
Christe. Vectes inferni potenter confregit ostesque ligauit.
Christe. Pendens in cruce proprio redemisti sanguine mundum.
Christe. Spineam ducens uertice coronam ipse pro nobis.
Christe. Teque uinciri uoluisti nosque a mortis uinculis eripuisti.

Kyrie. Qui latroni gaudia paradisi spondens donasti.
Parce iam mundi redemtor culpanti populo parce.
Kyrie. Qui de conuerso gaudio celos esse dixisti pie redemptor.
Kyrie. Viuens et regnans cum pater et sancto spiritu amen.

Translation:
Kyrie eleison. Lord have mercy.
Kyrie, Who came to suffer for us.

Translating Tradition

Kyrie, Who with outstretched hands have drawn all ages to yourself.

Kyrie, Who prophetically promised, "I will be your death, O death!"

Christe, Christ the Lord was made obedient even unto death — death on a cross.

Christe, Life dies on the wood [of the cross], the bite of hell is vanquished.

Christe, The bars of hell he broke mightily, and he bound the fiends.

Christe, Hanging on the cross you have redeemed the world by your own blood.

Christe, Wearing himself the thorny crown for us.

Christe, And you willed to be chained, and you delivered us from the chains of death.

Kyrie, Who, promising, granted the joys of paradise to the thief.

Spare now, Redeemer of the world, spare your sinning people.

Kyrie, Who said that the heavens rejoice over one repented sinner, merciful redeemer.

Kyrie, Living and reigning with the Father and the Holy Spirit amen.

Source: *Beneventanum Troporum Corpus 2: Ordinary Chants and Tropes for the Mass from Southern Italy*, A.D. *1000-1250* 1: *Kyrie eleison*, Recent Researches in the Music of the Middle Ages and Early Renaissance 19 (Madison: A–R Editions 1989) 38–41. For commentary see Recent Researches, vol. 20–21, pp. 99–104.

Chapter Two

The Bible in the Roman Rite

THE LATIN BIBLE?
LA declares that translators should refer to the *Nova Vulgata Editio,*
the post-Vatican II Latin Bible, "in order to maintain the tradition of
interpretation that is proper to the Latin liturgy" (24). The Council
of Trent is cited in support of this, but of course the Council of Trent
did not endorse the New Vulgate — it endorsed the old Vulgate.
No one who has actually studied the Nova Vulgata (=NV) could
possibly consider it a repository of traditional Latin exegesis or
interpretation, as "handed down by liturgical use and by the tradition of the Fathers" (41). Indeed, its very purpose was to eliminate
peculiarly Latin readings and interpretations, for the sake of conformity to the original Hebrew, Aramaic, and Greek, as the preferences of modern scholarship demand.[52] Thus the New Vulgate
differs from the traditional Vulgate in dozens if not hundreds of

---

[52] *Nova Vulgata Bibliorum Sacrorum Editio, Sacrosancti Oecumenici Concilii Vaticani II ratione habita, iussu Pauli PP. VI recognita, auctoritate Ioannis Pauli PP. II Promulgata* (Vatican City: Libreria Editrice Vaticana) Editio typica prior 1979, Editio typica altera 1986, Editio juxta editionem typicam alteram 1998. The 1986 and later editions include a "Praefatio ad Lectorem" and "Praenotanda" which explain the
principles of the translation. The intent was to stay closer to the traditional text
than was done in the Nova Versio of the psalter published by Pope Pius XII in
1945. However it seems to me that the translators' emphasis on continuity with
the Vulgate is overstated. For other views on the relationship of NV to the traditions of the Latin Bible, see: Tarcisio Stramare, ed., *La Bibbia "Vulgata" dalle origini
ai nostri giorni: Atti del Simposio Internazionale in Onore di Sisto V, Grottamare, 29–31
agosto 1985,* Collectanea Biblica Latina 16 (Rome: Abbazia San Girolamo, and
Vatican City: Librería Vaticana, 1987). Antonio García-Moreno, *La Neovulgata:
precedentes y actualidad* (Pamplona: Universidad de Navarra 1986).

places, some of them central to traditions of the Latin church.[53] Anyone who tries to read Latin ecclesiastical writings with the help of the *Nova Vulgata,* as I have, will soon despair, but she will despair all the quicker if what she is trying to do is unravel the Roman liturgy — not only because the NV leaves out much of the Vulgate, but because the liturgy employs much more than the Vulgate.

For example, the Easter introit presents Psalm 138[139]:18 as a prophecy of the resurrection: *Resurrexi et adhuc tecum sum,* "I have risen and still with you am I." This wording comes from the *Psalterium Romanum* or Old Roman Psalter, which is more ancient than the psalter of the Vulgate, called the *Psalterium Gallicanum* because of its popularity in Gallic regions. It is the Roman psalter that was the original psalm-text of the Roman rite, the source of most texts in the core repertory of Gregorian chant, and the source of much of the Roman Church's liturgical exegesis. Those of us who think we know better than to perceive christology in this verse, therefore, may initially feel relieved that the Gallicanum reads *exsurrexi et adhuc sum tecum* "I have stood up and still I am with you." But which reading better expresses the Latin tradition of interpretation? Consulting the fathers for guidance (as recommended in *LA* 41c) complicates matters very quickly: St Augustine's use of "exsurrexi" shows that this variant was in circulation even before the Vulgate — yet Augustine interprets it anyway as referring to the resurrection.[54] St Jerome's curiously named *Psalterium juxta Hebraeos* (much indebted to unacknowledged Jewish translations into Greek) helpfully parallels the Septuagint with "evigilavi," "I awoke."

But if we turn for guidance to NV, it isn't even close: *si ad finem pervenerim, adhuc sum tecum* "If I were to have arrived at the end,

---

[53] To take a prominent example, the traditional Vulgate of Genesis 3:15 says that the woman will crush the head of the serpent; hence almost every Catholic church displays an image of the Virgin Mary standing on a snake, expressing a major Latin exegetical tradition of Mary as the new Eve (also expressed in the medieval Latin palindrome "Ave Eva!" Cf. Revelation 12:1-17). But NV follows the Hebrew, in which it is the woman's son who will crush the snake. Strict application of *LA*'s principles, then, would require that all these statues be removed as antithetical to the Roman tradition!

[54] *Enarratio in Psalmum CXXXVIII*.25, ed. E. Dekkers and J. Fraipont in *CCL* 40 (1956) 2008.

still I am with you," meaning that we can never comprehend the mind of God. Thus NV rejects every reading known to have been sung, read or preached in the Latin church before the mid-twentieth century, and it does this for the very good reason that it aims to represent the original Hebrew.[55] Therefore, a translator who was considering a rendering like "'If I were done for' — I would still be with you!"[56] or "I am never finished with you,"[57] might feel compelled to follow the NV, perhaps with a more idiomatic "Should I arrive at the end. . . ." But she would be completely mistaken if she thought that she was thereby being "guided by the *Nova Vulgata* wherever there is a need to choose, from among various possibilities, that one which is most suited for expressing the manner in which a text has traditionally been read and received within the Latin liturgical tradition" (41a). She would in fact be rejecting the Latin liturgical tradition.

The NV is not alone here; the post-Vatican II liturgical books exhibit similar reluctance to follow the Latin liturgical tradition whenever it differs from the Hebrew Bible. For example, the current Roman Missal retains the Easter introit *Resurrexi* as the traditional one, but adds an alternative text that is a modification of a traditional Office antiphon: *Surrexit dominus vere, alleluia. Ipsi gloria et imperium per universa aeternitatis saecula.*[58] Such provision of an

[55] This reading originated in the new Latin psalter issued by Pope Pius XII, which says *si pervenerim ad finem.* The notes in that translation explain the Hebrew justification for this rendering, see *Liber Psalmorum cum Canticis Breviarii Romani: Nova e Textibus Primigeniis Interpretatio Latina cum Notis Criticis et Exegeticis Cura Professorum Pontificii Instituti Biblici Edita,* Editio Altera, Scripta Pontificii Instituti Biblici 93 (Rome: E Pontificio Instituto Biblico 1945) 292–93. The Confraternity translation of 1950 (incorporated into the New American Bible [=NAB] in 1970), based on the Hebrew as interpreted in the psalter of Pius XII, rendered this verse "did I reach the end of them, I should still be with you." But the revised NAB psalter of 1991 says "to finish, I would need eternity." For some reason the *Liturgia Horarum* psalter has *perveniam* ("I might arrive" or "I will arrive") instead of *pervenerim.*

[56] Hans-Joachim Kraus, *Psalms 60-150: A Continental Commentary,* trans. Hilton C. Oswald (Minneapolis: Fortress 1993) 510–11.

[57] *Christian Community Bible,* 27th ed. (Manila, the Philippines: Claretian Publications / St Pauls 1999) 1104. This translation is approved by the Catholic Bishops' Conference of the Philippines.

[58] The ICEL translation is "The Lord has indeed risen, alleluia. Glory and kingship be his for ever and ever." Luke 24:34 and Revelation 1:6 are cited as the

optional alternative alongside the objectionable original, however, is unusual. Less famous chant texts were simply replaced outright. For example, the previous verse of the same psalm (138 [139]:17), in both Roman and Gallican psalters, reads *Mihi autem nimis honorati sunt amici tui, Deus; nimis confortatus est principatus eorum,* "But to me your friends are greatly honored, O God; greatly strengthened is their pre-eminence." The Latin fathers identified these honored, princely friends of God with the apostles, an interpretation that was particularly valued in the see founded by Peter and Paul. As a result Psalm 138 was sung at the office on every feast of an apostle, with verse 17 supplying either introit, gradual, or offertory (or more than one) at the Mass of the day.

From NV, however, we learn that the original Hebrew verse was not about the friends of God, but about the thoughts of God: *Mihi autem nimis pretiosae cogitationes tuae, Deus; nimis gravis summa earum,* "But to me your thoughts are extremely precious, O God, extremely weighty the sum of them." Hence this verse is no longer to be found in connection with the apostles — or indeed anywhere in the renewed liturgy except the psalter for Week 4 of the Liturgy of the Hours. More was at stake than a translation change, however. The revisions made after Vatican II did not stop at eliminating outdated textual variants; they also eliminated "outdated" exegesis. Therefore all other psalm verses that ascribed princely status to the apostles were removed, even when NV did not change the traditional Vulgate wording: "With glory and honor you have crowned him" (Psalm 8: 6), and "You shall make them princes over all the earth" (Psalm 44[45]:17) were once typical apostle texts, but no more. An entire line of patristic exegetical thinking, which could not have been more Roman, has been systematically excised from the renewed Roman rite.

And the decision to eliminate such exegesis was not made casually. Biblical scholars today would consider it a distortion to imply that these psalms foretold the glory of the apostles, while many other people, for pastoral reasons, would approve the downplaying of royalty imagery (which is still used in the current liturgy for Christ, however, while Psalm 8 is in some places applied to the

---

sources. The 2002 *Missale* adds "alleluia alleluia" at the end. However *Surrexit Dominus vere, alleluia, et apparuit Simoni, alleluia* was an antiphon for Easter Monday.

human race as a whole). Catholic Biblical studies, in fact, has its own tradition of expressing polite horror at the age-old interpretations found in the liturgy. That is why Catholic Bible translations, even when made before Vatican II, contain footnotes warning the faithful not to believe the outrageous interpretations they will encounter in their worship: The slaughter of the Egyptian firstborn as foretelling Jesus' birth at midnight?[59] Ridicule of false prophets as Crucifixion typology?[60] I don't know how many people actually read these footnotes, but the authors of *LA* cannot be among them. Thus anyone trying to use the NV as a bridge to the Fathers will inevitably find themselves stuck at Luke 16:26: *inter nos et vos chaos magnum firmatum est. . . .*

The real question about the NV is why it even exists. Since its original purpose — to support modern liturgical celebrations in Latin (*Sacrosanctum Concilium* 91) — is largely hypothetical, it has until now served mostly as a placeholder, in the official Latin books, for Biblical passages that in practice would be supplied by vernacular translations. But since pope after pope has taught that the traditional Vulgate is free of doctrinal and moral error, why has it been thought necessary to change it? The underlying assumption seems to be that, one way or another, all texts of the revealed Word must ultimately say the exact same thing, and that this in turn must be the original Hebrew thing (or Aramaic or Greek). Textual variants, like sins, must be washed away. But if that is the case, why not go directly to the original Hebrew and Greek? *LA* has already warned us that "it is not permissible that the translations be produced from other translations already made" (24), but any translator who follows the NV will be doing precisely that. For all practical purposes, the NV is simply another modern translation.

---

[59] On the introit *Dum medium silentium,* still used in the Christmas season, see the footnote on Wisdom 18:15 in the New Jerusalem Bible.

[60] The "wounds in the middle of your hands" mentioned in Zechariah 13:6 were applied to the wounds of Jesus in readings and antiphons for the Votive Mass and Office of the Passion and for the feast of the Holy Lance and Nails. Thus in the Confraternity Version published before Vatican II, a footnote warns, "In the liturgy this text is applied to Christ in an accommodated sense." The services that contained the offending verse are now long gone, but the footnote remains in the New American Bible, the translation we now read in the liturgy!

Even if it is true that all versions of Scripture must ultimately conform to one original, one cannot without further ado ascribe this principle to the Fathers or "the tradition of the Latin church." The mere fact that Jerome's *juxta Hebraeos* (thought to be a literal translation from the Hebrew) was never put to liturgical use shows that Hebrew literalism was not considered a priority for Christian worship. Nor did it ever bother anybody to sing "Resurrexi" in the introit antiphon, "exsurrexi" in the accompanying psalm verse a few minutes later, then "Resurrexi" in the refrain again. When a difficulty was perceived, inspirational allegories could always be found to harmonize the diverse but not adverse discrepancies, as St Thomas did with the Credo. The basic principle of patristic and medieval exegesis, in fact, was that every sentence of Scripture had many interpretations: first the literal or historical, then a whole series of allegorical meanings, which foretell the Messiah, teach moral lessons, encourage the desire for heaven, and so on.[61] "The very multiplicity of possible true meanings hidden in the text of Scripture is proof of its providential origin, and of its authority as witnessing to the one Truth, which exceeds what any written text can contain."[62] Diversity, that is, affirms unity, on a deeper level than mere uniformity can.

And the case could readily be made that the modern cult of the Original is inconsistent with the Bible itself.

[61] The classic study is Henri de Lubac, *Medieval Exegesis: The Four Senses of Scripture*, trans. Mark Sebanc and E. M. Macierowski, 2 vols. (Grand Rapids, Michigan: W. B. Eerdmans 1998–2000).

[62] Brian E. Daley, "Is Patristic Exegesis Still Usable?" *Communio* 29/1 (Spring 2002) 185–216, see p. 199. See also Marie Anne Mayeski, "Quaestio Disputata: Catholic Theology and the History of Exegesis," *Theological Studies* 62 (2001) 140–53. For a modern use of typology, see Richard J. Clifford, "The Exodus in the Christian Bible: The Case for 'Figural' Reading," *Theological Studies* 63 (2002) 345–61. In 1993 the Pontifical Biblical Commission issued its authoritative statement, "The Interpretation of the Bible in the Church," which stated "The allegorical interpretation of scripture so characteristic of patristic exegesis runs the risk of being something of an embarrassment to people today. But the experience of the church expressed in this exegesis makes a contribution that is always useful" (III.B.2, final paragraph). The text is published with responses in J. L. Houlden, ed., *The Interpretation of the Bible in the Church* (London: SCM Press 1995), see p. 68. See also Joseph A. Fitzmyer, "Problems of the Literal and Spiritual Senses of Scripture," *Louvain Studies* 20 (1999) 134–46.

"The interpretation of the Bible goes back virtually as far as the oldest texts within it. Indeed, evidence of the process is to be found within the Hebrew Bible itself. Later Biblical books frequently mention or allude to things found in earlier books, and in so doing they often modify or change — sometimes radically — the apparent sense of the earlier text."[63]

Thus the New Testament authors were able to hear the Divine Word in the Septuagint,[64] in Aramaic paraphrases,[65] in punctuation changes and respellings of the Hebrew,[66] in allegory (Galatians 4:24), mistaken identities,[67] apocryphal and even unknown books.[68] Nor did early Christians refrain from "fixing" texts that, with the development of doctrine, came to seem unorthodox or embarrass-

---

[63] James L. Kugel, *Traditions of the Bible: A Guide to the Bible As It Was at the Start of the Common Era* (Cambridge, Mass.: Harvard University Press 1998) 2.

[64] Thus Isaiah's prophecy "the virgin shall conceive," to the endless consternation of fundamentalists Catholic and Protestant, has to be quoted from the Septuagint, since the original Hebrew word does not mean "virgin." See Raymond E. Brown, *The Birth of the Messiah: A Commentary on the Infancy Narratives in Matthew and Luke* (Garden City, N.Y.: Doubleday 1977) 144–50, 299–300.

[65] See, for example, Joel Marcus, "Rivers of Living Water from Jesus' Belly (John 7:38)," *Journal of Biblical Literature* 117 (1998) 328–30. Further examples will be found throughout Bruce D. Chilton, *A Galilean Rabbi and His Bible: Jesus' Use of the Interpreted Scripture of His Time*, Good New Studies 8 (Wilmington, Delaware: Michael Glazier 1984).

[66] Isaiah 40:3 is quoted in all four Gospels (Matthew 3:3 etc.) in a way that overlooks the original Hebrew parallelism, see James L. Kugel, *The Idea of Biblical Poetry: Parallelism and its History* (New Haven: Yale University Press 1981) 111–12. John 19:37 ignores a full stop in its quotation of Zechariah 12:10, according to the note on the Zechariah verse in the New Jerusalem Bible; another view is given in Raymond E. Brown, *The Gospel According to John (xiii–xxi)*, The Anchor Bible 29/2 (Garden City, N.Y.: Doubleday 1970) 938, 955–56. The Hebrew word for "bed" in Genesis 47:31 was repointed to spell "staff" in the sources of the Septuagint, and is quoted thus in Hebrews 11:21; see Harold W. Attridge, *The Epistle to the Hebrews*, Hermeneia — A Critical and Historical Commentary on the Bible (Philadelphia: Fortress Press 1989) 336.

[67] Matthew 13:35 and Mark 1:2 attribute to Isaiah quotations that are actually from other Old Testament books; these attributions were edited out of many manuscripts. Matthew 24:35 identifies the Zechariah of 2 Chronicles 24:20-22 with the author of the prophetic book of Zechariah, an error not made in Luke 12:51.

[68] James 4:5 gives a quote from "scripture" that is not to be found in any writing known today.

Translating Tradition

ing.[69] It is not my intent to challenge any dogmas here; I accept that the Church was right to exclude the Ascension of Moses and 1 Enoch from the canon, while accepting both the epistle of Jude, which quotes them as prophecy, and 2 Peter, in which these quotations have been edited out.[70] My point is that the traditional Roman liturgy resembles the canonical Scriptures in its capacity to hold competing models in creative tension, accepting "whatever is true, whatever is honorable, whatever is just, whatever is pure, whatever is lovely, whatever is praiseworthy" (Phil 4:8), while excluding whatever is genuinely incompatible with Christian revelation. LA's monochromatic invocations of Roman tradition seem completely unaware of this.

WITHOUT OMISSIONS, ADDITIONS, PARAPHRASES OR GLOSSES?

The differences between patristic and modern exegesis become particularly clear in LA's mistaken assumption that, to be true to the Roman rite, "the original text, insofar as possible, must be translated integrally and in the most exact manner, without omissions or additions in terms of their content, and without paraphrases or glosses" (20). I, too, would like to see translations more literal than some of the ones we use now. But to actually read the rich patrimony of the Roman rite is to discover that it did not insist on integral and exact textual renditions, while it did make use of omissions, additions, paraphrases, and glosses. This was partly due to the patristic approach to exegesis. But it was also because, before the invention of printing, people had a different conception of what the Scriptures actually were. The Bible for them was a living voice, heard in the oral proclamation of the readings, chanted in choir, expounded in preaching, meditated and ruminated while doing mundane work. The written manuscripts of the Bible, and the commentaries and sermons of the Fathers, existed to support this oral performance, not the other way round. Ultimately, it was

[69] Bart D. Ehrman, *The Orthodox Corruption of Scripture: The Effect of Early Christological Controversies on the Text of the New Testament* (New York: Oxford University Press 1993).
[70] Raymond E. Brown, *An Introduction to the New Testament,* The Anchor Bible Reference Library (New York: Doubleday 1997) 754–55, 759, 764–65.

The Bible in the Roman Rite

not in the letters seen on the page that people located the Bible, but in the act of hearing, as a direct encounter with what the words really meant. That is why, for them, there was no clear boundary between Scripture and Tradition. We can get some sense of this in the *Didascalicon* of the Augustinian Canon Hugh of St Victor. Written in the 1120s, it was one of the most popular textbooks of the Middle Ages.

"The whole of Sacred Scripture is contained in two Testaments, namely, in the Old and in the New. The books in each Testament are divided into three groups. The Old Testament contains the Law, the Prophets, and the Hagiographers; the New contains the Gospel, the Apostles, and the Fathers. . . .

"The first group of the New Testament contains four books: Matthew, Mark, Luke, and John. The second likewise contains four: the fourteen letters of Paul collected in one book; then the Canonical Epistles; the Apocalypse; and the Acts of the Apostles. In the third group, first place is held by the Decretals, which we call canons, or rules; the second, by the writings of the holy Fathers and Doctors of the church — Jerome, Augustine, Gregory, Ambrose, Isidore, Origen, Bede, and many other orthodox authors. Their works are so limitless that they cannot be numbered — which makes strikingly clear how much fervor they had in that Christian faith for the assertion of which they left so many and such great remembrances to posterity. Indeed, we stand convicted of indolence by our inability to read all that they could manage to dictate.

"In these groups most strikingly appears the likeness between the two Testaments. For just as after the Law come the Prophets, and after the Prophets, the Hagiographers, so after the Gospel come the Apostles, and after the Apostles the long line of Doctors. And by a wonderful ordering of the divine dispensation, it has been brought about that although the truth stands full and perfect in each of the books, yet none of them is superfluous. These few things we have condensed concerning the order and number of the Sacred Books, that the student may know what his required reading is."[71]

---

[71] Jerome Taylor, ed., *The Didascalicon of Hugh of St Victor: A Medieval Guide to the Arts*, Records of Civilization: Sources and Studies (New York: Columbia University Press 1961) 103–04.

Thus the pericopes of the traditional Roman lectionary were not simply cut and pasted out of a Bible, the way we do it today. They were deliberately modified to make them more suitable for oral liturgical performance, easier to apprehend and understand, and to incorporate elements of patristic interpretation into the text itself. Therefore many readings began with a brief introduction that, though not literally quoted from the Scriptures, was intended to establish a context for the story that those present were about to hear. Some readings were also adjusted at the end to give them a more appropriate liturgical closure. We can observe this kind of process in the way all ancient liturgies traditionally handled the Lord's Prayer, which of course is an excerpt from the gospel of Matthew (6:9-13). People did not simply begin at the words "Our Father." The priest introduced the prayer, in the Roman rite with *Preceptis salutaribus moniti . . .,* corresponding to "Let us pray with confidence" and other options in the modern English Sacramentary. After "deliver us from evil" the priest would continue praying, reciting a text liturgiologists call an embolism, which expanded on one of the themes from the prayer itself. Some traditions had a variable embolism, notably the Gallican rite. But the Roman rite used only one: *Libera nos . . .,* "Deliver us Lord from every evil." Today the most famous embolism of all is "For thine is the kingdom . . .," which developed in the Greek liturgical tradition and thus found its way into Greek manuscripts of the Gospel. From there, the great Reformation translations of the Bible reproduced it in fidelity to what they took to be the "original" Greek, with the result that it found widespread use in Protestant worship. It was finally introduced into the Roman Mass after Vatican II, though it had absolutely no precedent in the Latin fathers or the Latin liturgical tradition. There it serves as a congregational response to the priest's embolism, even though in its original Byzantine liturgical context, "For thine . . ." is the priest's embolism, not said by the congregation. Its present usage in the modern Roman missal, therefore, cannot be justified as preserving or restoring an ancient Roman tradition, but rather on the grounds that it gives the congregation one more text to say or sing in dialogue with the presider, and takes a step toward Christian unity in the text of the Lord's Prayer. It is one of many examples indicating why the present Roman Missal cannot simply be equated with the Roman tradition stretching back to the Fathers.

In the pre-Vatican II Roman Missal, the Epistles and Gospels had liturgical openings and closings that varied greatly. Some had only brief introductions of three words: *Haec dicit Dominus,* "Thus says the Lord" for Old Testament readings in which God is the speaker, *In diebus illis,* "In those days" for narratives, *In illo tempore,* "At that time" for Gospels. One still finds these sometimes in the current Latin lectionary, though they generally do not appear in the English lectionary (*LA* 45c demands their restoration). However, many readings in the pre-Conciliar rite had more extensive openings that identify the characters or the situation: "In those days the Lord spoke to Moses, saying," or "At that time Jesus said to his disciples," or "At that time Jesus said to the crowds this parable." These obviously helped prepare the listeners for what they were about to hear. But some of these openings go even further into actual paraphrase, like the Gospel that begins, "At that time Jesus spoke to the high priests and pharisees in parables, saying . . ." (Matt 22:1-14). This paraphrases a verse from the previous chapter (Matt 21:45), which properly belongs to a different parable; it is used here to supply a context, since the pericope itself does not specify whom Jesus was addressing.[72] In another case, a reading from the book of Jeremiah began, "In those days the impious Jews said to each other," preceding the actual beginning of the pericope, "Come, let us plot against the just one . . ." (Jer 18:18). The prophet characteristically responded to these murmurers with a prayer asking God to destroy and refuse to forgive them, ending with the words "in the time of your anger, waste them!" (18:23). But the Missal adds three extra words after this, *Domine Deus noster,* "O Lord our God" — a stock liturgical closing that was generally used to finish off jeremiads and prophetic prayers. In the oral context of the liturgy, this helped signal that the reading had come to an end (the acclamation "The word of the Lord" that we use now is another Vatican II innovation), and it helped the listeners keep the characters straight by clarifying that the speaker was a human addressing God. Thus it was not perceived as adding anything foreign to the Biblical text, as it would seem now with our more literate, visual orientation.

[72] The Gospel in this case is that of the nineteenth Sunday after Pentecost.

Such additions did more than identify context and characters, though: they also introduced elements of interpretation, which in turn made connections to broader contexts of liturgical time and space. In this case, the reading of Jeremiah occurred on the Saturday at the end of Passion week (i.e., the day before Palm Sunday), when themes of opposition and betrayal were increasingly being emphasized. This doubtless influenced the description of the prophet's opponents as "impious Jews," a phrase that is not in the Bible. But it even prompted a subtle yet important change in the scriptural text itself, for in the Bible the murmurers say, "Let us plot against Jeremiah." The liturgical reading "Let us plot against the just one," though departing from the literal text, made it clear typologically that the passage was not merely about some Old Testament prophet, but foreshadowed the betrayal of Jesus, the truly Just One. More than that, the deliverance that the just one prays for in this reading was foreshadowed in the very building where this pericope was read at the stational Mass that day: the church of St John before the Latin Gate, where the evangelist survived boiling in oil in a failed attempt to martyr him.[73] The change from "Jeremiah" to "the just one," then, was not a merely superficial variant, but was deliberately designed to bring out rich exegetical associations with the New Testament, the liturgical season, and the physical space. I do not know whether the authors of LA would classify it as an omission, addition, paraphrase or gloss, but I am sure it is just the sort of thing they would forbid, since it changes the Biblical text. In doing so, however, they would be departing from, not embracing, the kind of exegesis practiced by the Fathers. That is because they do not think of the liturgy in the patristic way, as an action, in which humans speak and listen and interact within a holy space, in the presence of Someone greater than the prophets (cf. Matt 12:6, 41-42 and parallels). No, they think, in the modern way, that the liturgy is a text written in a book, a text that quotes other texts. From that perspective, the omissions, additions, glosses and paraphrases of the traditional Roman Missal look like violations of the Bible's integrity. For the Fathers, and all premodern Catholics, changing "Jeremiah" to "the just one" was not

---

[73] Hartmann Grisar, *Das Missale im Lichte römischer Stadtgeschichte: Stationen, Perikopen, Gebräuche* (Freiburg: Herder 1925) 31.

The Bible in the Roman Rite

altering the text, but only bringing out the Bible's real meaning, as St Jerome made clear: "When I read the Gospel and I see there testimonies from the law, testimonies from the prophets, I consider only Christ. I have seen Moses in such a way, have seen the prophets in such a way, that I understand them to be speaking of Christ. When I finally come to the splendor of Christ and have looked upon it as the most radiant light of a bright sun, I am not able to see the light of a lamp. If you light a lamp in the daytime, can it shine? If the sun is shining, the light of the lamp is not visible. So, too, compared with Christ being present, the law and the prophets are not visible. I do not detract from the law and the prophets — rather I praise them all the more because they preach Christ. But as a result I read the law and the prophets so that I will not remain in the law and the prophets, but through the law and the prophets come to Christ."[74]

Whoever changed "Jeremiah" to "the just one" was looking through the prophets to see the light of Christ, in the true Roman and patristic way, not altering the text but opening up a deeper meaning. If this seems strange to us, it is a measure of how distant we are from reading the Bible as the Fathers did. One of the major causes of this distancing was the invention of printing in the fifteenth century. The undeniable gain of Gutenberg's new idea was that it made it possible for everyone to own his own Bible, without spending years to copy it out by hand. But every historical advance brings with it both gains and losses, and the drawback of having cheap mass-produced Bibles was that the Bible itself changed, from a living voice, lovingly proclaimed and sung and enacted in the liturgy, to a mere book, consulted and argued about and returned to the shelf.

Indeed, when the Roman Missal was revised after the Council of Trent, the medieval oral sensibility was already losing ground to the modern literate sensibility, and some of the editorial introductions were cleaned up as a result. One of them is of particular interest to us since it involved a gender switch. The epistle on the Wednesday after the second Sunday of Lent began "In those days

---

[74] *Tractatus in Marci Evangelium* 9.1-7, ed. G. Morin, CCL 78 (1958) 484, quoted with approval by Benedict XV in his 1920 encyclical *Spiritus Paraclitus*, see *Acta Apostolicae Sedis* 12 (1920) 418–19.

Esther prayed to the Lord, saying. . . ." This made Esther recite a prayer that, in the Bible, is said by Mordechai (Vulgate 13: 8-11, 15-17 = NAB 4C: 1-4, 8-10). Thus in the first "Tridentine" edition of the Missal, issued by Pope Pius V in 1570, it was corrected to say "Mordechai prayed," as if it had been a mere mistake. But the Esther attribution was not an anomaly — it had been included in every Roman liturgical book since the earliest extant epistolary, from the seventh century.[75] And it was not an error, or it would have been corrected centuries before Pius V. Re-attributing the prayer to Esther made possible a typological parallel with St Cecilia, the patron of the stational church in which this text was read.[76] As with the application of Psalm 138 to the Apostles, and the parallelism of Jeremiah with Jesus and St John, this way of inter-connecting typology with hagiography and stational liturgy was a distinctly Roman approach to the Bible, not found in this form in the other Latin liturgical traditions, and different from the approach used (for example) in the stational lectionary of Jerusalem. It was a major factor in shaping the classic Roman Missal — I suggest calling it "hagiological typology." At its most potent, it could and did justify massive rewriting of Biblical texts.

Thus the epistle "Ecce sacerdos magnus" for feasts of popes (the source of several chant texts, set to music hundreds of times) is an extensive rewrite of three chapters from the book of Sirach (Ecclesiasticus), turning his praise of Jewish high priests into a more fitting description of an ideal Christian pontiff (see Appendix B, p. 56). It is not just a matter of a few variant readings or a liturgical introduction, but of substantive additions and omissions, paraphrases and glosses, making the liturgical reading say things the Bible (as we read it) simply does not say. Few people today, liberal or conservative, would accept such a text as a genuine reading from the Bible, yet this epistle cannot be dismissed as an aberration: It is found in every single Roman book, from the earliest epistolary[77] through the Missal of 1962. This means that anyone who has permission to use the 1962 Missal is still reading it with

[75] Germain Morin, "Le plus ancien comes ou lectionnaire de l'église romaine," *Revue Bénédictine* 27 (1910) 41–74, see p. 51, number LIII.

[76] Grisar, *Das Missale* 29–30.

[77] Morin, "Le plus ancien *comes*" p. 47, number XVI.

Vatican approval — and that, once again, scrupulous obedience to *LA* would result in absurdity. The majority of Catholics who have accepted liturgical renewal would be compelled to abide by *LA*'s rigid and unforgiving model of textual quotation, justified as preserving the traditions of the Roman rite, while those who reject liturgical renewal altogether, in favor of the historic Roman rite, would continue to read seventh-century omissions, additions, paraphrases and glosses.

A renewed study of the Roman liturgical sources could provide us with a powerful model of the orally proclaimed Scriptures, sung and preached within the worshiping community, linking liturgical time and space. If, in spite of that, Roman officials insist on imposing a visual, two-dimensional, printed-book model of Scripture as more suitable to the way we think today, this should be presented honestly as the modernization it actually is, not as preserving a Roman tradition which in historical reality knew no such thing. But to acknowledge the difference would encourage those who, convinced by pastoral experience, believe that Bible texts sometimes need to be modified for effective liturgical use — this was a wisdom that the ancient Roman rite already possessed. A translator who changes wording to make the real meaning clearer, therefore, is not *ipso facto* violating the Roman liturgical tradition. Even if higher officials prudently decide that her proposed modifications cannot be approved for use, it would be unjust to accuse the translator of trying to create a new rite. No qualified translator is demanding the power to rewrite the Scriptures at whim, just as no ecclesiastical authority may construe tradition at whim. The tradition itself offers us the poisonous image of "impious Jews," to warn how easy it is to read our own preconceptions into the Bible and proclaim them in the liturgy. But the real moral of the story is this: our contemporary conflicts become easier to solve when charitable dialogue is honest and fully-informed about what the sources of tradition actually reveal. For what they reveal is a diversity that is not adverse, a diversity that ultimately affirms a unity deeper than uniformity.

We can learn even more if we compare the Roman approach of "hagiological typology" to the procedures followed in other Eastern and Western traditions. The Gallican rite, for example, made use of harmonies or centos, combining verses from all four

Gospels to tell a fuller story of such pivotal events as the Nativity or Passion of Christ.[78] This was never done at Rome, and many would not accept it today. But if it should prove useful in some future situation, let no one say, as the LA authors seemingly would, that it violates the Latin liturgical tradition. Indeed the Latin liturgical tradition is even broader than this, for among its diverse but not adverse witnesses there is also an approach that does somewhat resemble LA's literalistic ideal, though it is carefully marked off as un-Roman. In the ninth century, as the Gallican rite was being suppressed (by the emperors, not the popes), the French primatial see of Lyon adopted a then-unique approach to the liturgical use of Scripture. At the behest of its feisty bishop Agobard and the deacon Florus, every reading and chant text in the Lyon Mass and Office was revised to conform literally to the standard Vulgate of the time, with all additions and rewordings removed. Over the centuries, the diocese maintained this commitment to scriptural exactness, and renewed it several times during local reforms, jealously preserving it in part because of the distinctiveness it provided in contrast to the Roman rite. From Lyon the model was adopted by the Carthusian order, as more in keeping with its austere lifestyle than the Roman approach.[79] The papacy never interfered, and the Lyon and Carthusian rites were ancient enough to be exempted from the Tridentine reforms. All this is in marked contrast to Agobard's other agendas, such as his ferocious opposition to image veneration, allegorical interpretation, and "the insolence of the Jews." Even the local Lyon tradition came to

---

[78] Pierre Salmon, ed., *Le lectionnaire de Luxeuil (Paris, ms. lat. 9427):* 1: *Édition et Étude comparative: contribution à l'histoire de la Vulgate et de la liturgie en France au temps des mérovingiens,* Collectanea Biblica Latina 7 (Rome: Abbaye Saint-Jérome; Vatican City: Liberia Vaticana 1944) CIV–CXXIII.

[79] Augustin Devaux, *Les origines du missel des chartreux,* Analecta Cartusiana 99:32 (Salzburg: Institut für Anglistik und Amerikanistik, Universität Salzburg 1995) 26–27. See also Emmanuel Cluzet, *Particularités du missel cartusien,* 5 vols., Analecta Cartusiana 99:26–99:31 (Salzburg: Institut für Anglistik und Amerikanistik, Universität Salzburg; Lewiston, N.Y.: Edwin Mellen Press 1994). Cluzet, *Sources et genèse du missel cartusien,* Analecta Cartusiana 99:34 (Salzburg: Institut für Anglistik und Amerikanistik, Universität Salzburg 1996). Kazimierz Szymonik, "Gradual Kartuzów: Studium zródloznawcze," *Muzyka religijna w Polsce: Materialy i studia* 2, ed. Jerzy Pikulik (Warsaw: Akademia Teologii Katolickiej 1978) 273–357.

The Bible in the Roman Rite

dismiss these as merely his personal viewpoints, and did not retain them as distinctive features of the Lyon rite. The combination as a whole earned Agobard a unique historical trajectory, as he bounced precipitously from a seventeenth-century stint on the Index of Forbidden Books to an eighteenth-century berth in the local Lyon calendar of saints, twice approved by popes.[80]

Only in the nineteenth century did the Neo-Gallican controversy finally force Pope Pius IX to interfere with the Lyon rite, along with other French diocesan uses. In a nineteenth-century missal that I have examined, there are glosses and interpolations, but they are scrupulously set off from the Vulgate text by means of square brackets.[81] But the basic validity of the Lyon rite was reaffirmed by Pius's successor Leo XIII, who promptly restored it, at least in part. Only after Vatican II expressed a new openness to liturgical diversity did the Lyon rite fade away, and this local church now uses the same Roman Missal and Lectionary as everyone else, supplemented by a local calendar. But for over a thousand years — through the Great Schism, the Counter-Reformation, the French Revolution, Neo-Gallicanism and everything else — the rite of Lyon fulfilled an important prophetic function, ensuring that the bishop of Rome presided over a church in which differing, locally-based models of liturgical Scripture proclamation flourished side by side in peace.

ONE APPROVED TRANSLATION?

I agree with *LA* (36) that the use of a standard common text would help congregations learn and remember the Bible, particularly the

---

[80] On the Lyon rite see Denys Buenner, *L'Ancienne liturgie romaine: Le rite lyonnais* (Lyon: E. Vitte 1934); Archdale A. King, *Liturgies of the Primatial Sees* (London: Longmans, Green 1957) 1–154; Robert Amiet, *Inventaire général des livres liturgiques du diocèse de Lyon* (Paris: Éditions du Centre National de la Recherche Scientifique 1979); Amiet, *Les manuscrits liturgiques du diocèse de Lyon: Description et analyse* (Paris: CNRS Éditions 1988).

[81] *Missale Sanctae Lugdunensis Ecclesiae, Primae Galliarum Sedis* (Lyon: Rusand 1825). According to a newspaper clipping that accompanies the Georgetown University copy, this missal was still being used during the First World War, when an American soldier rescued it after a church was bombed during a Mass he was attending. One might have expected that the priest would be using the Vatican-approved *Missale Romanum in quo antiqui ritus Lugdunenses servantur* of 1904 (see Amiet, *Inventaire*, pp. 125–26).

Psalms. But its notion that "there should exist only one approved translation" has never been a principle or practice in the Roman rite, least of all for the Psalter. If it were put into effect it would, in fact, be a dramatic departure from the Roman tradition. We have already seen that there were three major texts of the Psalms in Latin: the Roman, the Gallican or Vulgate, and Jerome's *juxta Hebraeos*. Often in medieval manuscripts (known as "triple psalters") the three main texts have been copied side by side in parallel columns to support comparison. Some MSS have more than three columns, since there were also Milanese, North African, Hispanic text types and more. The rest of the Bible, too, circulated in multiple Latin translations, which scholars now refer to collectively as the Old Latin versions or *Vetus Latina*. These versions were never completely supplanted by the Vulgate, and particularly not in the liturgy; to study the history of Latin liturgy and chant, therefore, I have to have every one of them on my shelf.

The oldest layers of the Gregorian chant repertory (seventh through ninth centuries) usually follow the Roman psalter, sometimes other non-Vulgate texts. The pericopes of the Roman lectionary, which are first attested in the seventh century, represent a tradition that reflects both Vulgate and Old Latin readings, which has therefore been dubbed "the Latin liturgical text" by the only Biblical scholar I know of who has actually studied it.[82] In the oral environment of the liturgy, variant readings could circulate for centuries, even without the help of written sources, just as we still pray "forgive us our trespasses" with William Tyndale's 1526 translation, 400 years after the Geneva, Douay-Rheims and King James versions agreed on the more Latinate "debts."

The survival of so much non-Vulgate material in the liturgical tradition was due not only to oral transmission, but also to the simple fact that, even in the darkest ages, readers knew the Latin

---

[82] See the following works of William J. Gochee: "The Gospel Text of the Latin Liturgy: A.D. 400–800" (PhD diss., University of Chicago 1970); "The Latin Liturgical Text: A Product of Old Latin and Vulgate Textual Interaction," *Catholic Biblical Quarterly* 35 (1973) 206–11; "A Textual View of the Struggle of the Early Medieval Church in the West," *Traditio - Krisis - Renovatio aus theologischer Sicht: Festschrift Winfried Zeller zum 65. Geburtstag,* ed. Bernd Jaspert and Rudolf Mohr (Marburg: N. G. Elwert 1976) 81–91; "Some Observation [sic] on the Operation of the Monastic Scriptorium," *Scriptorium* 31 (1977) 242–46.

Bible was a translation; the studious liked to compare translations, just as some English readers do today. It was not just a matter of bibliophilia, however, it was a matter of papal policy — for the popes have generally supported the best biblical scholarship available in their time, as long as it was not presented in terms of a challenge to the faith. Pope Gregory the Great stated as much in the preface to his *Moralia in Job,* the great example of tropological or moral exegesis. "I base my discussion on the new translation, but when the need to prove something demands it, I take sometimes the new, sometimes the old as witnesses; because the Apostolic See, over which I preside by God's design, uses both, and also the labor of my study is supported by both."[83] By "the new translation" Gregory meant the Latin Vulgate, then almost 200 years old.

Pope Gregory died in 604. Exactly a thousand years later, another pope reaffirmed that a multiplicity of Bible versions was to remain the policy of the Apostolic See. The endorsement of the Vulgate by the Council of Trent had not entailed the suppression of competing Latin translations or their banishment from the liturgy,[84] but there were people in the decades following the Council who thought it should have. Many publishers took the obvious step of issuing missals in which all chants and readings had been replaced by the corresponding Vulgate segment, particularly after Pope Clement VIII issued his new edition of the Vulgate in 1592 (the *Editio Clementina* would remain the standard Vulgate into the twentieth century). Yet Clement himself rejected these new missals. In 1604 he issued his own *Missale Romanum,* restoring the non-Vulgate chant texts and the traditional, textually-modified pericopes to the form in which Pius V had published them in 1570. His bull explaining all this, *Cum sanctissimum,* is easy to find, for it was reprinted in every subsequent edition of the Roman Missal up through 1962. "Since the most holy Sacrament of the Eucharist, in which Christ the Lord has made us partakers of his own sacred Body, and also resolved to remain with us even to the consummation of the world, is the greatest of all sacraments, and is confected in the sacred Mass, and offered to God the Father for the sins of the whole people — surely

[83] *Moralia in Job,* Epistula Leandro 5, ed. M. Adriaen in *CCL* 143 (1979) 7.
[84] Tanner, *Decrees* 2: 664, 723, 797.

Translating Tradition

it is wholly appropriate that we who are all one in one body, which is the Church, and who partake of the one Body of Christ, should use one and the same rule of celebrating, by observing one office and rite in this ineffable and awe-filled sacrifice. Therefore, as the Roman Pontiffs our predecessors always desired, and long exerted themselves in this and much else, so Pope Pius V of happy memory especially endeavored to have the Roman Missal published in Rome, restored to the old and more corrected norm by decree of the sacred Tridentine Council. Though he severely stipulated with many proposed penalties that nothing be added to it, or cut out for any reason, nevertheless with the passing of time, the temerity and boldness of publishers and other people have brought it about that many errors have crept into the Missals which have been printed in recent years. Among them: that oldest version of the Bible, which they had in the Church even before the times of the celebrated Saint Jerome, and from which almost all the Introits of the Mass and so-called Graduals and Offertories were received, has been completely removed; the text of the Epistles and Gospels, which was read out up to now in the ceremonies of the Mass, [has been] disturbed in many places; differences [have been introduced] in these same Gospels, and completely unaccustomed beginnings prefixed to them; finally many things throughout [have been] changed at will. The pretext for this seems to have been that everything should be brought back to the standard of the Vulgate edition of the sacred Bible, as if it were lawful for someone to do this by his own authority, and without consulting the Apostolic See. Therefore, taking note [of all this] because of our pastoral solicitude, we strive to protect and conserve the best and the same old norm in all things, and especially in the sacred rites of the Church. We have commanded, first, that the aforesaid printed Missals, which are so depraved, be prohibited and abrogated, and their use in the celebration of Mass be forbidden, unless they be emended integrally and in all things to the standard of the exemplar published under the same Pius V. . . ."

Certainly, Clement's model was one of uniformity as the best expression of unity — though he was also the pope who had permitted the Ukrainian "Greek Catholics" to retain their Byzantine rite at the Union of Brest-Litovsk in 1596. And Clement's brand of uniformity was one rigidly enforced from above, for the bull goes

on to excommunicate anyone who prints a Missal outside the Papal
States without a license from "our beloved sons, the inquisitors of
heretical depravity," or where there was no inquisitor the local
ordinary. But Clement's ideal of uniformity was a paradoxical one,
emphatically not based on a common Bible text. Instead of following the trend of the times by imposing his own Vulgate, Clement
re-imposed scriptural disunity as "the best and the same old
norm" that had been followed immemorially. Nor did he do this
because he was under the impression that he lacked authority to
alter the text of Pius V. Clement's 1604 missal was no mere reprint,
but a new if modest revision, and the bull describes the commission of cardinals he convened to carry it out. They added some new
feasts and a new chapter of rubrics on the construction and orna-
mentation of altars, and somewhat expanded the available models
of female sanctity by adding a Common of Non-Virgin Martyrs.
Even in an age, then, when the church was at its most defensive,
with hierarchical structures of obedience widely accepted, papal
directives promptly carried out, the inquisition only too happy to
help, at just the historical moment when there was a new Vulgate
edition to conform to and editors eager to do the job, a pope
expressly rejected the possibility of imposing one uniform Bible
text on the liturgy. Today we no longer use his Missal, his Bible, or
his methods (for the most part). But what stronger proof could
there be that using "only one approved translation" is not a traditional principle of the Roman rite?

CENTURIES OF ECCLESIAL EXPERIENCE?
What *LA* actually demonstrates is how thoroughly the liturgical reform has effaced — even in Rome itself — the memory of what the
Roman liturgical past was like. For despite all its protestations about
fidelity to tradition, *LA* is remarkably uninformed about the history
of the Roman and Latin liturgical traditions. Its authors are not
familiar with the treatment of Greek and Semitic words in the Latin
Scriptures and liturgies. They are unacquainted with the history of
the Credo and the *Kyrie;* they use Aquinas as a source of proof texts
without regard for what he was actually saying. They do not understand the relationship between the *Nova Vulgata* and the traditional
Vulgate, and seem unaware of the other Latin Bible texts used in the
Roman tradition. They show no sign of ever having read any patristic

exegesis. They do not know that paraphrases, glosses, and textual adaptations have existed throughout the history of the Roman Mass lectionary and chantbooks, or that the other Latin rites followed their own alternative approaches. They are not conversant with any editions of the Missal prior to Paul VI. They are unacquainted with basic information that, in 1900 or 1950, would have been considered common knowledge among liturgical specialists.

Instead, *LA* presents a nearly-fundamentalist view of the liturgical texts currently in force. Whatever is in the approved books today (no matter how or when it got there) is the Roman rite by definition, not only juridically but even historically. Since the current books are the Roman rite, they can simply be equated with the Latin liturgical tradition (singular rather than plural), and must therefore represent whatever the Latin Church Fathers taught (the *LA* authors themselves have not read the Fathers). The result is a kind of telescoped liturgical history in which nothing ever really changed: "The Latin liturgical texts of the Roman Rite, while drawing on centuries of ecclesial experience in transmitting the faith of the Church received from the Fathers, are themselves the fruit of the liturgical renewal. . . . In order that such a rich patrimony may be preserved and passed on through the centuries, it is to be kept in mind from the beginning that the translation of the liturgical texts of the Roman liturgy is not so much a work of creative innovation as it is of rendering the original texts faithfully and accurately . . ." (20).

Contrast this with the words of one of the original leaders of the liturgical reform, writing at a time when many people could still remember the liturgy before Vatican II: "Let's make no mistake: translating does not mean saying the same thing in equivalent words. It changes the form. And liturgy is not just information or teaching, whose only importance is its content. It is also symbolic action by means of significant 'forms'. If the forms change, the rite changes. . . . We must say it plainly: the Roman rite as we knew it exists no more. It has gone. Some walls of the structure have fallen, others have been altered; we can look at it as a ruin or as the partial foundation of a new building."[85]

---

[85] Joseph Gelineau, *The Liturgy Today and Tomorrow*, trans. Dinah Livingstone (New York: Paulist Press 1978) 11.

But we cannot honestly look at it as simply unbroken continuity, as if the liturgical renewal merely cleaned up a few details. Some walls fell of their own accord; others were pushed. And this was not done out of some irrational hatred of Roman orthodoxy, but because the Roman liturgical tradition, at least as it was understood and practiced in the early twentieth century, was no longer communicating much of its richness to many modern Christians, with our higher rates of literacy and increasingly democratic civil society, our daily and weekly schedules altered by economic forces, our modern worldview brought about by science and technological change that has revolutionized travel, home life, warfare, indeed almost everything. The discrepancy between the potential and the reality looked even larger in light of all that centuries of liturgical scholarship had revealed about what the liturgy had once been, so that the desire understandably grew strong to, once again, have a liturgy fully connected to Christian life. Those who do not remember can gain a sense of what this desire felt like by re-reading the words of another leader of the liturgical movement who, indulging in some allegorical interpretation of his own, compared the liturgy to the treasure hidden in the field (Matt 13:44-46): "Another such treasure, and truly one of great price, in the field of the Church is the Holy Sacrifice; yet for so many Christians it lies buried and unappreciated. Those of us who long to live with the Church and to offer sacrifice with her, we have found this treasure, and our one concern now is to lay hold of it and make it our own."[86]

No doubt the authors of *LA* would agree. Yet reading what they have written does not feel like finding a treasure in a field. Wisdom says, "Cry out for insight and raise your voice for understanding, . . . seek it like silver and search for it as for hidden treasures" (Prov 2:3-4). *LA* speaks as if there is nothing left to search for: the field has been walled in and paved over, the treasures are all fully excavated, catalogued, and safely stored in the Vatican museum, and we are to buy only the licensed reproductions available in the museum shop. But the promise of liturgical renewal was supposed to be that we could "lay hold of it and make it our own," and if there is one thing all Catholics can agree on, I think it is that the work of "making it our own" remains unfinished, even woefully

---

[86] Pius Parsch, *The Liturgy of the Mass,* third ed., translated and adapted by H. E. Winstone (London and St Louis: B. Herder 1957) xiii.

unfinished. Much of that work belongs to what we now call "inculturation," a subject so complicated that it will require another chapter to respond to what *LA* has to say about it.

Meanwhile, I think there is a better metaphor for the Catholic liturgical tradition than the treasure hidden in the field. St Isidore of Seville (died 636), who wrote the first treatise in Latin on the Christian liturgy, is often described as the last of the western Church Fathers. He was very aware of his position as the heir to a great tradition, and in a poem he wrote to post on his bookcases he compared his own vast library to a garden.

"There are many sacred things here, there are many worldly things here.
From these, if any songs [carmina] are pleasing, take up, read.
You see fields full of thorns, and rich with flowers.
If you do not wish to take the thorns, take the roses.
Here gleam the venerable volumes of the double law;
Stored here equally are the New [Testament] with the Old."[87]

It is a rare privilege to be able, almost every day, to take up and read the pleasing songs of the Latin church and the Roman rite, in libraries far larger than Isidore could have imagined. To those of us who are fortunate enough to be in this position, the tradition is indeed like a huge garden, filled with great trees that grew from tiny seeds, lilies that neither toil nor spin, weeds that will not be uprooted till the end of time. The beautiful jostles the useful, the medicinal shares soil and water with the poisonous, insects cross-pollinate the future while compost and dung heaps recycle the past. It is like being the bride in the Song of Songs: "I went down to the walnut grove to see the fruits of the valley, and to see whether the vine had blossomed, whether the pomegranates were in flower. I was amazed — my soul set me among the chariots of my princely people" (6:11-12).[88]

---

[87] *Versus qui in Bibliotheca sancti Isidori episcopi Hispalensis legebantur* 1, ed. PL 83:1107, now ed. José María Sánchez Martín in CCL 113A (2000) 213.

[88] In the spirit of *diversi, non adversi* I have taken advantage of several minority Christian and Jewish opinions on the rendering of this difficult verse. See Marvin H. Pope, *Song of Songs: A New Translation with Introduction and Commentary,* The Anchor Bible 7c (Garden City: Doubleday 1977) 552, 584–92; Shmuel Yerushalmi, *The Book of Shir HaShirim,* trans. Zvi Faier, Me'am Lo'ez (New York: Moznaim 1988) 278–81; Karlfried Froehlich, "'Aminadab's Chariot': The

But *LA*'s authors do not express any sense of wonder or awe toward the Roman tradition. It brings them no joy, because they do not really know it. Reading what they have to say makes me want to cry out the bride's complaint, "My mother's children were angry with me; they made me guard the vineyards; but my own vineyard I did not guard" (Song 1:6). The tradition blossoms with potential, *LA* bristles with impossibilities. The tradition is bursting with vitality, *LA* is rigid with prohibitions. With a tradition as ancient, complex, and variegated as the Roman rite, why would anyone choose the thorns over the roses?

Appendix B

Epistle reading in *Missale Romanum*, 1962 ed.	Medieval Vulgate sources, from Ecclesiasticus (Sirach) except where noted
Lectio libri Sapientiae.	
Ecce	Simon Onii filius
sacerdos magnus, qui	**sacerdos magnus qui** in vita sua suffulsit
in diebus suis	domum et **in diebus suis** corroboravit
placuit Deo, et	(50:1)
inventus est justus, et in tempore	Noe **inventus est** perfectus **justus et in**
iracundiae factus est reconciliatio.	**tempore iracundiae factus est**
	reconciliatio (44:17)
	Abraham magnus pater mulitudinis
	gentium et
Non est inventus similis illi, qui	**non est inventus similis illi** in gloria **qui**
conservavit legem Excelsi.	**conservavit legem Excelsi** (44:20)
Ideo jurejurando	**ideo iureiurando**
fecit **illum** Dominus	dedit **illi** semen
crescere in plebem **suam.**	**in** gente **sua crescere**
	illum quasi terrae cumulum (44:22)
Benedictionem omnium gentium dedit	**benedictionem omnium gentium dedit**
illi, et testamentum suum **confirmavit**	**illi et testamentum confirmavit super**
super caput ejus.	**caput** Iacob (44:25)
Agnovit eum in benedictionibus suis:	**agnovit eum in benedictionibus suis** et
	dedit illi hereditatem et divisit ei partem
	in tribus duodecim (44:26)

Predicament of Biblical Interpretation," *Princeton Seminary Bulletin* new series 18 (1997) 262–78; Graham S. Ogden and Lynell Zogbo, *A Handbook on Song of Songs*, UBS Handbook Series (New York: United Bible Societies 1998) 189–90.

conservavit illi misericordiam suam: et invenit gratiam coram oculis Domini.	et conservavit illis homines misericordiae invenientes gratiam in oculis omnis carnis (44:27)
Magnificavit eum	et magnificavit eum in timore inimicorum . . . (45:2)
in conspectu regum:	glorificavit illum in conspectu regum . . . (45:3)
et dedit illi coronam gloriae.	et dedit illi coram praecepta legem vitae et disciplinae . . . (45:6)
Statuit illi testamentum aeternum, et dedit illi sacerdotium magnum: et beatificavit illum in gloria. Fungi sacerdotio, et habere laudem	statuit ei testamentum aeternum et dedit illi sacerdotium gentis et beatificavit illum in gloria (45:8) fungi sacerdotio et habere laudem et glorificare populum suum
in nomine ipsius, et offerre illi incensum dignum in odorem suavitatis.	in nomine suo ipsum elegit eum ab omni vivente adferre sacrificum Deo incensum et bonum odorem. . . . (45:19-20) in odorem suavitatis (Ephesians 5:2, cf. Genesis 8:21)

Translation of the liturgical reading:

A reading from the Book of Wisdom.

Behold, a great priest, who in his days pleased God, and was found just; and in the time of wrath he was made a reconciliation. There was not found the like to him who kept the law of the most High. Therefore, by an oath the Lord made him to increase among his people. He gave him the blessing of all nations, and confirmed his covenant upon his head. He acknowledged him in his blessings; he preserved for him his mercy; and he found grace before the eyes of the Lord. He glorified him in the sight of kings, and gave him a crown of glory. He made an everlasting covenant with him, and gave him a great priesthood: and made him blessed in glory. To execute the office of the priesthood, and to have praise in his name, and to offer him a worthy incense for an odor of sweetness.

Source: "Common of a confessor bishop," in *The Epistles and Gospels: Extra Large Type Edition, Printed from Hand-Set Type* (New York: William J. Hirten Company 1941) 42c–43c.

Chapter Three

Languages and Cultures

Some of the problems we have with worship today arise from the
tendency to see inculturation and tradition as opposites: either one
does something the traditional way, or one adapts it to a modern
culture. Thus people feel compelled to take sides, favoring one
over the other. Much trouble could be avoided by learning to see
tradition and inculturation as two sides of the same coin, or two
perspectives on the same phenomenon — for tradition is the
record of inculturations past, a storehouse of models and resources
for inculturations today, which in turn will generate the traditions
of the future. It was possible to see this even before Vatican II,
when the word "inculturation" had not yet been invented. Thus
Thomas Merton could write: "There is a difference between a
mystery and a dogma. A dogma of the faith is a more abstract,
authoritative statement of the truth to be believed, couched in its
official formulation. . . . A mystery is not just the distilled and
decanted formulation of a revealed truth, but that whole truth in
all its concrete manifestation: in the mysteries of the faith we see
God Himself, generally in one of those great theandric actions in
which He has revealed Himself to us in a concrete and tangible
form. . . .

"To meditate on a mystery of the faith in this sense means first
of all to perceive it externally as it is presented to us, as part of the
Church's experience. The Church's experience of the mysteries
. . . is handed down from age to age in tradition. Tradition is the
renewal, in each Christian generation and society, of the experiential knowledge of the mysteries of the faith. Each new age of Christendom renews its faith and its grasp of the mystery of salvation,
the mystery of man united to God in Christ, and each age renews

this fundamental experience of the Christian mystery in its own characteristic way.

"To enter into the mysteries of the faith by meditation, guided by the spirit of the Church, especially by the spirit of the liturgy and of Christian art, is to renew in oneself the Church's experience of those mysteries by participating in them. And of course the full participation of the Christian in the mystery of Christ is sacramental, public, liturgical: in the sacraments and at Mass. Hence the close relationship between private meditation and the public worship of the Church."[89]

This is why there can be diversity without adversity: the same incarnate Word is with us all days, making disciples of all nations.

Thus the relationship between tradition and inculturation should be one of balance and discernment, avoiding the two extremes that would sacrifice one to the other: One extreme would see the local culture as a problem to be overcome on the way to thorough Romanization, which should be achieved by keeping changes in the liturgy to the necessary minimum. The other extreme would locate most of the problems in the tradition, ready to jettison anything that makes teenagers yawn. A more reasonable and accurate view would recognize that, in the real world, culture and tradition are interconnected symbiotically. Thus for people in traditionally Christian societies, the liturgy and its arts form a major and inextricable part of cultural heritage. And in most if not all societies, cultural elements that have died out in secular life still survive in the religious celebrations of community and sacrifice, initiations, weddings, and funerals. We can see this in our own culture in such practices as "giving the bride away," which many modern women would not go through if they thought they were endorsing its original social meaning. Indeed, there is no better illustration of the inherently conservative character of liturgical worship than the strange fact that the Roman Catholic Mass (of all things) has become the last bastion of late 1960s folk-rock, long after popular music has moved on through disco, house, techno and trance, rap and hip hop.

[89] Thomas Merton, *Spiritual Direction and Meditation* (Collegeville: The Liturgical Press 1960) 84–86, italics original.

The preservation of heritage and cultural diversity are thus important human goods, even human rights. That is why Vatican II taught that Christians are obligated to make all people "aware of their right to culture, as well as of their responsibility to cultivate themselves and help others do the same," because "the human person . . . can attain to real and full humanity only through culture."[90] The systematic destruction of Tibet's culture now being carried out by the occupying Chinese government provides abundant confirmation of the truth of this neglected Conciliar teaching.

In the Catholic liturgy, therefore, issues like translation, inculturation, and the safeguarding of traditions are not mere procedural issues, but potentially ethical ones. It would nowadays be difficult to justify a liturgical regime that denied the importance of cultural diversity by preventing people from worshiping in their native language and forms of cultural expression. But it should be equally difficult to justify an approach so detached from tradition that it prevents people from experiencing or appreciating the vast legacy of Christian liturgical and artistic expression. Both diversity and heritage are vulnerable to misguided efforts at "inculturation," regardless of whether the fantasies being enacted are liberal or conservative ones. In parts of Europe, for instance, old local traditions of congregational song and rural folk polyphony have unaccountably been washed away by a flood of pseudo-folk songs mimicking the American "folk mass."[91] I have observed this myself, for example, in St Mark's cathedral in Venice, which once housed one of the most important musical traditions of any building in Europe. There I watched slack-jawed as one of the canons struggled hopelessly to teach a congregation to sing "Kum ba ya"

---

[90] *Gaudium et spes* 60, 53, trans. Tanner, *Decrees* 1110, 1106.

[91] Though there has not been a lot of research on these developments, see: Ludovic Tournès-Fortin, "La culture de masse à l'église? L'introduction avortée de la musique noire américaine dans la liturgie catholique française (1960–1970)," and Hervé Rivière, "Des timbres et de l'hymnodie catholique bretonne entre les conciles Vatican I et Vatican II," *Le chant, acteur de l'histoire: actes du colloque tenu à Rennes, du 9 au 11 septembre 1998*, ed. Jean Quéniart (Rennes: Presses Universitaires de Rennes 1999) 265–78, 307–21. Emil Čić, "Das zweite Vatikanum und die liturgische Idee über die sacrale Musik in Kroatien," *International Review of the Aesthetics and Sociology of Music* 29 (1998) 75–90.

in Italian ("Sei con noi, Signor . . ."). Though the same people had absolutely no trouble, after the service was officially over, belting out the entire Litany of Loreto — in Latin and from memory — I have always wondered if the good priest went home pondering the mystery of why Catholics cannot sing.

Back in the U.S.A., meanwhile, we inhabit a spirituality market-place in which it is much easier to find books and workshops about enneagrams and yoga (helpful as they may be for some people) than about praying the psalms, interpreting Christian iconography, making an examination of conscience, reading the lives of the saints. It should be no surprise, then, that this situation has spawned its own antithesis — the emergence of a vengeful "conservatism" unencumbered by history, promoted by grassroots groups doing all they can to obscure what remains of our sense of continuity with our religious forebears by spreading joyless, uncharitable messages all over the Internet.

Of course, much of the problem is coming from powerful forces outside the church. The more interconnected world of today, with its high valuation of individual autonomy, does raise important questions about the continuing value of specifically Western and Christian cultural traditions: slogans like "cultural literacy," "diversity," and "political correctness," are crude pointers to some of them. But we Christians should advocate our own values within these debates, not abdicate leadership to other entities pursuing their own self-interests. The global advertainment industry, for instance, has obliterated quite a lot of cultural memory in the effort to direct people's cultural needs toward its own proprietary products, which in turn are carefully crafted to promote the sale of even more products. Endlessly factionalized public education is not helping either. When students in my religious education classes tell me they do not know any songs older than last year's pop hits, or that St Patrick is a leprechaun who helps people find pots of gold, I wonder if any previous generation has ever known so little about the tales and traditions of its ancestors, or if, indeed (an eschatological portent no less dreadful), the snakes have come back to Ireland. When they tell me that Christmas is about the primeval battle between Generosity and Selfishness, whose mythi-cal avatars walk the earth as Santa and The Grinch, I can only respond with the trademarked question: What Would Jesus Do?

Languages and Cultures

At the college level, where I spend more of my time, I regularly meet people of every and no religious background who have learned to love Catholic traditions of art or music, literature or philosophy, but cannot understand why, if they were to visit an actual Catholic church — even many university chaplaincies — they would rarely find anyone who values, or has even heard of, the individuals and artifacts they find so fascinating and spiritually enriching. No branch of American Judaism, by contrast, would be comfortable with this degree of cultural amnesia. A refueling stop at the oasis of *liturgia authentica* would be a most salubrious thing.

TRUE INCULTURATION?

Thus the new Vatican document *Liturgiam Authenticam* (*LA*) takes a positive step in asking us to see the Roman rite as both "a precious example and an instrument of true inculturation" (5), a way of worshiping that brings us into communion with all the past generations and cultures whose experience of the Christian mystery helped to shape this tradition. The implementation of Roman liturgical practices by non-Roman Christians — some willing, others unwilling — has been going on since at least the early fifth century, when Pope Innocent I sent to the bishop of Gubbio a list of Roman customs to follow.[92] All that has happened since then, a millennium and a half during which numerous cultures adopted and adapted the Roman rite, offers us a huge panorama of stories, examples, and cautionary tales that have everything to do with the issues we wrestle with today. The problem is that much of this history is still little known and barely researched. The sheer number of languages involved is an obstacle in itself, but another reason is our tendency to classify anything historical as "tradition," and nothing that happened before our time as "inculturation." Because we associate inculturation with innovation, we have barely begun to think about formulating the research questions that need to be asked of the historical sources. And the field of liturgiology in its present form, because of its own particular history, is (to use Merton's distinction) better equipped to deal with dogmas than with mysteries; more about this farther on.

[92] Cabié, ed., *La lettre du pape Innocent Ier.*

Even before modern times, history shows that a variety of approaches to inculturating the Roman rite has been tried, with differing results. Among the earliest and best known is the replacement of the Gallican rite by the eighth-century Frankish kings Pepin and Charlemagne, an example of inculturation by adaptation.[93] "The Franco-German clergy did not look upon their new liturgy as a treasure which was not to be meddled with and which they merely had to pass on. . . . [D]uring the eighth and ninth centuries, the Franks boldly developed the liturgy they had inherited, exercising at the same time a high degree of creative ability."[94] By contrast, the introduction of the Roman rite into Slavic lands, beginning in the ninth century, offers a model of inculturation as translation, along with a history of competition with the Byzantine rite that ultimately dominated most worship in the Slavonic language.[95] The eleventh-century reconquest of Spain from the Moors brought with it Cluniac monks who supplanted the local Mozarabic liturgy with the newly hybrid Frankish-Roman rite — inculturation by conquest.[96] Indeed the Spanish never forgot their native Mozarabic rite, and found a variety of strategies to keep it going in limited ways. A form of it, renewed since Vatican II, is still celebrated in a special chapel of the cathedral of Toledo. In the eighteenth century the Mozarabic rite was even taught to seminarians in New Spain, though they presumably would never have the opportunity to celebrate it.[97]

[93] Yitzhak Hen, *The Royal Patronage of Liturgy in Frankish Gaul to the Death of Charles the Bald (877)*, Henry Bradshaw Society Subsidia 3 (London: Boydell Press 2001).

[94] Klauser, *A Short History of the Western Liturgy*, 78.

[95] Cyril Korolevsky, *Living Languages in Catholic Worship: An Historical Inquiry*, trans. Donald Attwater (London: Longmans, Green 1957) 73–95; Angelus A. De Marco, *Rome and the Vernacular* (Westminster, Maryland: Newman Press 1961) 35–53.

[96] Damian J. Smith, "Sancho Ramírez and the Roman Rite," *Unity and Diversity in the Church*, ed. R. N. Swanson, Studies in Church History 32 (Oxford: Blackwell 1996) 95–105. How the change is reflected in liturgical manuscripts from the period is explored in Rose Walker, *Views of Transition: Liturgy and Illumination in Medieval Spain*, The British Library Studies in Medieval Culture (London: The British Library, and Toronto: University of Toronto 1998).

[97] *Missa gothica seù mozarabica, et officium itidèm gothicum, diligentèr ac dilucidè explanata ad usum percelebris Mozàrabum sacelli Toleti . . .*, ed. Francisco Antonio

The inculturation of the Roman rite among the new world peoples of the Americas is one of the greatest stories never written. Huge quantities of documents survive in both European and Amerindian languages, but much remains unexamined, even uncatalogued. A major element in this effort was the teaching of European types of music to the native Americans, with the result that (for example) Baroque instruments and techniques that have died out in Europe are still used today by Latin American Indians, side by side with more indigenous music.[98] In the Jesuit missions of Caughnawaga or Kahnawake in Quebec, and St Regis in New York State, the Gregorian chant melodies for the Ordinary of the Mass were sung to Mohawk texts, so that at least some North Americans were singing the Kyrie in translation *(Takwentenv Sewenniio!)*[99] before Vatican I — possibly even before the American Revolution.[100]

The history of the Syriac rites in India constitutes a veritable encyclopedia of Catholic, Protestant, and Eastern approaches to inculturation — with absolutely no consensus as to whether or not any of them actually "worked." Better known is the Chinese rites controversy, which raged for centuries. Along with issues of language was the question: could Christianity be inculturated so

---

Lorenzana y Butrón and Francisco Fabian y Fuero (Angelopoli [=Puebla, Mexico]: Typis Seminarii Palafoxiana 1770).

[98] Frank and Joan Harrison, "Spanish Elements in the Music of Two Maya Groups in Chiapas," *Selected Reports in Ethnomusicology* 1/2 (1968) 1–44; Frank L. Harrison, "Music and Cult: The Functions of Music in Social and Religious Systems," *Perspectives in Musicology: The Inaugural Lectures of the Ph.D. Program in Music at the City University of New York*, ed. Barry S. Brook et al. (New York: W. W. Norton 1972) 307–34, especially 321–22, 325–26, 333; Frank Harrison, "Tradition and Acculturation: A View of Some Musical Processes," *Essays on Music for Charles Warren Fox*, ed. Jerald C. Graue (Rochester, N.Y.: Eastman School of Music Press 1979) 114–25.

[99] Western Americana MS S-2190 in Yale University's Beinecke Library, a Caughnawaga manuscript dating from the 1850s through the 1890s, contains multiple musical settings of the Mass Ordinary, the Dies irae, and other liturgical chants with texts in Mohawk. Interestingly, the Ite missa est and its reply were not translated, only transliterated *(Teoo krasiiaas!)*.

[100] I have not been able to confirm that this was permitted "thanks to concessions obtained by Jesuit missionaries in the 17th century," as stated in C.R.A. Cunliffe, "Liturgical Languages," *New Catholic Encyclopedia* (New York: McGraw-Hill 1967) 8:897–99, see p. 899 column a.

Translating Tradition

deeply as to adopt Confucian ceremonies honoring the dead? Yet the large literature on this tends to focus on the debates between Europeans. Conditions in China are not yet favorable for extensive investigation of the Chinese side of the experience.[101]

There is, as I said, much we could learn from these stories. But there is no trace of them in LA. Its tales are much stranger, the like of which has never been heard. If LA's account of the Roman liturgical tradition could be described politely as "parahistorical" (though plenty of published research is readily available), its view of inculturation history (where the published research is much more preliminary) is positively fanciful. In this respect it continues what I think has been the most problematic aspect of liturgical renewal generally, a pervasive unawareness that there is anything to be learned from the social sciences about language, culture, or community. Or perhaps a fear, common to partisans of many stripes, that one's own liturgical agenda is just too important to be entrusted to experts. Nowadays we expect that ecclesiastical statements on medical ethics will be up-to-date on the biological facts, that statements on Scripture will be fully informed about current biblical scholarship. Indeed the pope consults with a Pontifical Academy of Sciences and a Pontifical Biblical Commission. Yet liturgical practices and policies imposed on millions of worshipers have often been based on little more than conventional assumptions and offhand personal impressions. LA provides all the demonstration we need that much contemporary theorizing and policy-making about liturgical inculturation is taking place in an informational vacuum, as if theology or canon law were all one needed to know.

PEOPLES EVANGELIZED LONG AGO?

Thus LA asks us to remember a time when the Roman rite was a dominant force in the shaping of language and culture. "Liturgical

[101] See, for example, Ray R. Noll, ed. *100 Roman Documents Concerning the Chinese Rites Controversy (1645–1941)*, trans. Donald F. St Sure (San Francisco: Ricci Institute for Chinese-Western Cultural History 1992). Some Chinese viewpoints are presented along with many Western ones in D. E. Mungello, ed., *The Chinese Rites Controversy: Its History and Meaning*, Monumenta Serica Monograph Series 33 (Nettetal, Germany: Steyler Verlag 1994). On the use of the Chinese language see also De Marco, *Rome and the Vernacular* 55–76.

translation that takes due account of the authority and integral content of the original texts will facilitate the development of a sacral vernacular, characterized by a vocabulary, syntax, and grammar that are proper to divine worship, even though it is not to be excluded that it may exercise an influence even on everyday speech, as has occurred in the languages of peoples evangelized long ago" (47, see also 59). Try as I might, though, I cannot figure out what historical period or language(s) they are talking about. When and where did liturgical translation of the Roman rite create a sacral vernacular that even shaped everyday speech? I wondered, for example, if they were referring obliquely to a controversy that took place recently in Spanish-speaking countries, encapsulated by the differences in connotation between the pronouns "ustedes" and "vosotros." If so they are mistaken, for expressions like these probably come from aristocratic court ceremonial; their "Latin" antecedents (*vestras mercedes, *vos alteros) do not occur in the liturgy. The sermons of the Latin fathers address the congregation with different formulas, derived from Latin epistolary conventions.[102]

After all, most of the "peoples evangelized long ago" were worshiping in Latin up to about 1965. To my knowledge, pre-modern translations of the Roman rite exist only for languages in which the Roman rite was actually celebrated: Greek, Slavonic, and Armenian.[103] Translations of the liturgical books, even for private study, were generally forbidden from at least 1661 to 1875.[104] Before

[102] Mary Bridget O'Brien, *Titles of Address in Christian Latin Epistolography to 543 A.D.*, The Catholic University of America Patristic Studies 21 (Washington, D.C.: The Catholic University of America 1930).

[103] Charles M. Atkinson, "Further thoughts on the origin of the 'Missa Graeca,'" *"De musica et cantu": Studien zur Geschichte der Kirchenmusik und der Oper: Helmut Hucke zum 60. Geburstag*, ed. Peter Cahn and Ann-Katrin Heimer, Musikwissenschaftliche Publikationen 2, (Hildesheim: Olms 1993) 75–93; De Marco, *Rome and the Vernacular* 77–80; Gabriele Winkler, "Armenia and the Gradual Decline of its Traditional Liturgical Practices as a Result of the Expanding Influence of the Holy See from the 11th to the 14th Century," *Liturgie de l'Église particulière et liturgie de l'Église universelle: Conférences Saint-Serge, XXIIe Semaine d'études liturgiques, Paris, 30 juin - 3 juillet 1975*, Bibliotheca Ephemerides Liturgicae Subsidia 7 (Rome: Edizioni Liturgiche 1976) 329–68. Unpublished Armenian translations of Roman liturgical books still exist in medieval manuscripts.

[104] For the prohibitions, see *Decreta Authentica Congregationis Sacrorum Rituum et Instructio Clementina ex Actis Ejusdem Collecta*, ed. Aloisius [= Luigi] Gardellini and

the liturgical movement, people who could not read Latin were not given translations but paraphrases, frequently in poetry. One can see them in the books that were used to teach lay people what to do during Mass, such as the *Lay Folks Mass Book*.[105] The medieval priests who wrote such books did not aim to give lay readers a literal understanding of what the clergy and choir were saying, but to tell them when to stand, kneel, etc., and to elicit appropriate devotional feelings of contrition, reverence, thanksgiving, and so on at the appropriate points during the service. Yet many copies contain handwritten interpolations which show that their lay owners did not always use the texts as intended, revealing a "devotional underground" that medieval clergy regarded as superstitious, where prayer seemed to be about bargaining with higher powers for safety from misfortune and the redress of grievances.[106] In fact the spiritual formation of the laity was, as we shall see, a very complicated problem in the Middle Ages. What historical documents reveal is quite unlike *LA*'s picture of liturgical language molding vernacular speech. But it is not even possible to discuss the history without understanding three major issues in the study

Wolfgang Mühlbauer 2 (Munich: J. J. Lentner 1865) 262–63; Supplementum 2 (Munich: Ernst Stahl 1879) 564–66. The Sacred Congregation of Rites began deferring the matter to individual bishops in the 1870s, see *Decreta Authentica Congregationis Sacrorum Rituum ex Actis eiusdem Collecta eiusque Auctoritate Promulgata sub Auspiciis SS. Domini Nostri Leonis Papae XIII* 3 (Rome: Typographia Polyglotta, S. C. de Propaganda Fide 1900) p. 61, no. 3373 (4 Sept. 1875); p. 82, no. 3427 (4 Aug. 1877); pp. 328–29, no. 3950 (20 Mar. 1897). The first definitive indication that the prohibition had been dropped was the fact that it was not mentioned in the apostolic constitution *Officiorum ac munerum* of Pope Leo XIII (1897), which revised the rules on forbidden books. On the remarkable historical situations that brought about the prohibition of 1661, see Louis Bouyer, *Liturgical Piety* (Notre Dame, Indiana: University of Notre Dame Press 1955) 51–52.

[105] Thomas Frederick Simmons, ed., *The Lay Folks Mass Book, or The Manner of Hearing Mass with Rubrics and Devotions for the People . . . from Manuscripts of the Xth to the XVth Century*, Early English Text Society 71 (London: Oxford University Press, 1879, repr. 1968).

[106] Virginia Reinburg, "Popular Prayers in Late Medieval and Reformation France," (PhD dissertation, Princeton University 1985), especially chapter 4. See also Paul Post, "John Bossy and the study of liturgy," *Omnes circumadstantes: Contributions towards a history of the role of the people in the liturgy presented to Herman Wegman*, ed. Charles Caspers and Marc Schneiders (Kampen: J. H. Kok 1990) 31–50.

of linguistics that *LA* completely overlooks: language stratification, language contact, and language change.

Language stratification. A document that invokes patristic authority as much as *LA* does should exhibit some awareness that the church fathers carried on an extended debate over the relative advantages of educated vs. popular styles of language.[107] One end of the spectrum is represented by St Jerome's dream in which the Divine Judge condemned him because "You are a Ciceronian, not a Christian"[108] — the other by St Augustine's question: Why should not "good and zealous Christians" acquire oratorical skill "to fight for the truth, if the wicked employ it in the service of iniquity and error?"[109]

Even in the classless United States there are significant differences in vocabulary, pronunciation, and "discourse strategies" between people of different social and economic backgrounds.[110] Such differences are, of course, even more pronounced in unabashedly hierarchical societies, so that a greengrocer's daughter

---

[107] Erich Auerbach, *Literary Language & Its Public in Late Latin Antiquity and in the Middle Ages*, trans. Ralph Manheim, Bollingen Series 74 (Princeton University Press 1965); Ernst Robert Curtius, *European Literature and the Latin Middle Ages*, trans. Willard R. Trask, Bollingen Series 36 (New York: Bollingen Foundation 1953, repr. Princeton: Princeton University Press 1990) 40–41, 46, 216, 449; Pierre Riché, *Education and Culture in the Barbarian West from the Sixth through the Eighth Century*, trans. John J. Contreni (Columbia: University of South Carolina Press 1976) 79–99; Jacques Fontaine and Charles Pietri, eds., *Le monde latin antique et la Bible*, Bible des tous les temps 2 (Paris: Beauchesne 1985) 25–42, 129–52; Carol Harrison, "The Rhetoric of Scripture and Preaching: Classical decadence or Christian aesthetic?" *Augustine and his Critics: Essays in Honour of Gerald Bonner*, ed. Robert Dodaro and George Lawless (London: Routledge 2000) 214–30; Adam Kamesar, "Ambrose, Philo, and the Presence of Art in the Bible," *Journal of Early Christian Studies* 9 (2001) 73–103.

[108] *Epistula* 22.30 *Ad Eustochium*, ed. I. Hilberg in *Corpus Scriptorum Ecclesiasticorum Latinorum* 54 (1910) 190.

[109] *De Doctrina Christiana* 4.5, ed. R.P.H. Green, Oxford Early Christian Texts (Oxford: Clarendon Press 1995) 198–99.

[110] William Labov, *The Social Stratification of English in New York City* (Washington, D.C.: Center for Applied Linguistics 1982); John J. Gumperz, *Discourse Strategies*, Studies in Interactional Sociolinguistics 1 (Cambridge: Cambridge University Press 1982); Deirdre Boden and Don H. Zimmerman, eds., *Talk and Social Structure: Studies in Ethnomethodology and Conversation Analysis* (Cambridge: Polity Press 1991).

like Margaret Thatcher had to take lessons in elocution to begin
the political career that made her the elected leader of the United
Kingdom. Medieval societies were even more intensely stratified,
with those on the bottom supporting not one but two hierarchies
of privilege: the aristocratic and the ecclesiastical. Understanding
this is crucial to evaluating phenomena like the vernacular tropes
(properly called *farses*) which, in twelfth-century France, were
interpolated into the epistles during the octave of Christmas. Since
these poetic stanzas are in early Romance dialects, we are naturally
inclined to perceive them as early harbingers and across-the-ages
vindication of Vatican II, representing a first feeble effort to convey
to the unschooled laity what the Latin epistles were saying. The
farses may even remind us of the more ancient Aramaic targums
of the Old Testament, which also are not literal translations, for
"If the Romance stanzas do not constitute a real translation of the
Latin verse, they assure its intelligibility."[111] However, a recent
study concludes that their function was almost the opposite of
what we would like: preserving clerical control over areas of worship (such as the Christmas octave) where pre-Christian or secular
elements of the culture were most likely to emerge. Though such
uses of the vernacular evidently produced "a lexical enrichment of
the Romance language" by contributing "calques, latinisms, and
cultisms," it was less a matter of the people worshiping in their
own tongue than of the clergy speaking to them *juxta rusticitatem*.[112]

Medieval clergy had good reason to be concerned about popular
expressions of lay spirituality, as we shall see. But the ability of
priests to use lay language for their own purposes is an example of
what linguists call *register* or *stylistic variation*. Even illiterate
speakers generally understand that differences in vocabulary, pronunciation, syntax and so on make a style of language appropriate
(or not) to a specific situation or environment.[113] This is the reason

[111] Yvonne Cazal, *Les voix du peuple — Verbum Dei: Le bilinguisme latin - langue
vulgaire au moyen âge*, Publications romanes et françaises 223 (Geneva: Librairie
Droz 1998) 65.

[112] Cazal, *Les voix du peuple* 310, 308.

[113] For an introduction to this phenomenon see Douglas Biber, Susan Conrad,
and Randi Reppen, *Corpus linguistics: Investigating language structure and use*,
Cambridge Approaches to Linguistics (Cambridge: Cambridge University Press
1998) 135–71. For a variety of opinions on how it operates see Nikolas Coupland

historians rarely have access to what *LA* calls "everyday speech" from any period before the invention of sound recording in the late nineteenth century. Before then we are entirely dependent on written texts, which were usually written for some purpose that called for a more formal or at least non-colloquial register. There are very few writings we can point to and say with confidence, "This is what everyday speech was like."

Language contact. Contact Linguistics is a massive and complex field that finds its material in many parts of the world. In general "it has been shown that languages in contact can affect one another at every level — phonetic, phonological, syntactic, semantic, idiomatic, and even morphological." However, "the agency for this process is a population of bilinguals, significant either in proportionate numbers or in prestige and influence. The real locus of language 'contact' is the mind of the bilingual individual."[114] That would mean that whatever influence liturgical Latin exerted on the vernacular did not take place among the monoglot laity, but among the clergy who knew both languages and possessed "prestige and influence." In fact the vernacular literature that actually survives from the Middle Ages tends to confirm this, even though it is often difficult to reconstruct its original social context. When we find vernacular tongues in contact with liturgical Latin, it generally fits into one of three situations: 1) texts written by clergy for lay audiences, e.g., sermons, commentaries, devotional and hagiographical literature,[115] 2) texts used by low-level clergy and female religious who were not fully at home with the sacred

---

and Adam Jaworski, *Sociolinguistics: A Reader*, Modern Linguistics Series (New York: St Martin's Press 1997) 163–265.

[114] Colin P. Masica, "Areal Linguistics," *International Encyclopedia of Linguistics*, ed. William Bright (Oxford: Oxford University Press 1992) 1:108-112, quote from 110. For more detail, see: Monica Heller, ed., *Codeswitching: Anthropological and Sociolinguistic Perspectives*, Contributions to the Sociology of Language 48 (Berlin: Mouton de Gruyter 1988); Pieter Muysken, *Bilingual Speech: A Typology of Code-Mixing* (Cambridge: Cambridge University Press 2000); Carol Myers-Scotton, *Contact Linguistics: Bilingual Encounters and Grammatical Outcomes* (Oxford: Oxford University Press 2002).

[115] One detailed study of this vast topic is: Michel Zink, *La prédication en langue romane avant 1300*, Nouvelle bibliothèque du moyen âge 4 (Paris: Honoré Champion 1976).

Translating Tradition

language, and thus used some mixture of the two, 3) literary works by highly-educated laymen who knew Latin well, such as Dante, Chaucer, or Villon.[116] While it may be that Latin expressions filtered down from these venues into the speech of illiterate lay people, this is not so easy to document.

For our topic there is an added complexity, however, because in the medieval period it is not so easy to delineate exactly what we mean by "Latin." There was the Latin of the liturgy, the Latin of the law courts, the Latin of patristic writings, the Latin of the classical authors.[117] But there is also the crucial question: when did medieval speakers begin to perceive a difference between Latin and the emerging Romance languages? Some would say that it is the Romance dialects that stand in true historical continuity, through Vulgar Latin, with the Latin of classical times, and that the Latin of the medieval church was an artificial language, whose grammar and pedagogy was largely established by non-Romance speakers: the Celts, Anglo-Saxons and Germans who learned Latin as a foreign tongue and wrote the medieval Latin grammars.[118] On the other hand, even in a place like Britain, which had never fully been conquered by the Romans, a spoken "Book Latin" that was not Romance may have persisted longer than we know.[119]

Finally, languages and societies differ as to whether and how to accept outside influences. We can readily see this by looking at the distribution of Christian calendric terminology. Since most Western Europeans ultimately came to follow the Roman liturgical calendar, common sense would suggest that the influence of the

[116] Evelyn Birge Vitz, "The Liturgy and Vernacular Literature," *The Liturgy of the Medieval Church*, ed. Thomas J. Heffernan and E. Ann Matter (Kalamazoo: Western Michigan University 2001) 551–618.

[117] F.A.C. Mantello and A. G. Rigg, *Medieval Latin: An Introduction and Bibliographical Guide* (Washington, D.C.: Catholic University of America Press 1996).

[118] See the articles in Roger Wright, ed., *Latin and the Romance Languages in the Early Middle Ages*, 2nd printing (University Park: Pennsylvania State University Press 1996) especially 1–5, 103–11; Jószef Herman, *Vulgar Latin*, trans. Roger Wright (University Park: Pennsylvania State University Press 2000) 109–23.

[119] Alfred Wollman, "Early Christian Loan-Words in Old English," *Pagans and Christians: The Interplay between Christian Latin and Traditional Germanic Cultures in Early Medieval Europe*, ed. T. Hofstra et al., Germania Latina 2 (Groningen: Egbert Forsten 1995) 175–210; Alfred Wollman, "Early Latin Loan-Words in Old English," *Anglo-Saxon England* 22 (1993) 1–26.

liturgical language would be pervasive here. But it is not. Most European languages still name the days after the seven planets of ancient astronomy, preserving the Babylonian astrological week as it was popularized in the late Roman Empire. Church leaders campaigned to replace this system with the simple ordinal numbers found in Genesis 1 and in the liturgy, with Monday the "second feria," Tuesday the "third feria," and so on.[120] Yet only Portuguese fully adopted the Biblical/liturgical enumeration; Icelandic and a few others did so partially. Spanish, French and Italian accepted "Sabbath" and "Lord's day" for Saturday and Sunday, but retained the planetary names for the weekdays. English and German not only kept the planetary week, but even replaced most of the Greco-Roman names with parallel Norse deities.[121] We find similar variety in the names of holidays. Despite massive exposure to both Latin and Norman French, we English speakers still use pagan Germanic names for Lent and Easter, and have not forgotten Yule.[122]

In fact, the treatment of foreign words is one of the variables by which languages differ.[123] Detailed study of the three major early Germanic dialects shows that each took its own approach to naming Christian concepts. Gothic, for instance, was much more accepting of Christian loan words (from Greek) than Old English or Anglo-Saxon, which tended to "baptize" pagan words rather than borrow (from Latin). Old High German, meanwhile, seems to have borrowed its Christian vocabulary from Old English — not

[120] For an example of ecclesiastical preaching against the astrological names, see William E. Klingshirn, *Caesarius of Arles: The Making of a Christian Community in Late Antique Gaul*, Cambridge Studies in Medieval Life and Thought, Fourth Series (Cambridge: Cambridge University Press 1994) 233–34.

[121] Sun-day, Moon-day, Tiw's day (=Mars), Woden's day (=Mercury), Thor's day (=Jupiter), Frigga's day (=Venus), Saturn's day (no Germanic equivalent). See Eviatar Zerubavel, *The Seven Day Circle: The History and Meaning of the Week* (New York: The Free Press 1985) 5–26; E. G. Richards, *Mapping Time: The Calendar and its History* (Oxford: Oxford University Press 1998) 391–97; Bonnie Blackburn and Leofranc Holford-Stevens, *The Oxford Companion to the Year* (Oxford: Oxford University Press 1999) 566–68.

[122] On the terminology of days and seasons, see Blackburn and Holford-Stevens, *The Oxford Companion to the Year* 516, 608, 621, etc.

[123] Winfred P. Lehmann, *Historical Linguistics: An Introduction*, 3rd ed. (London: Routledge 1992) 264–78.

Translating Tradition

surprising since German speakers received the faith from Anglo-Saxon missionaries like St Boniface.[124] The end result was that each language developed its own distinctive Christian terminology. The English word Christmas ("Christ's Mass") combines two anglicized Latin words in a way that Latin itself would not: "*Christi Missa" is not a Latin expression, and if it did occur it would not necessarily imply the feast of the Nativity.[125] German *Weihnachten* ("in the consecrated nights"), which may be a holdover from the pre-Christian winter solstice celebration, uses non-Latin words to create a term that has no direct Latin counterpart.[126] Even something as culture-shaping as the Roman liturgical calendar, then, did not simply colonize the vernacular languages and bend them all to Roman ways; on the contrary, it challenged each tongue to respond according to its own native genius.

Language change. Living languages change. Even if there was a time when liturgical Latin was a dominant social force that shaped the vernaculars in contact with it, this would not necessarily mean that we could return to that relationship now, or that the "sacral vernacular" created back then would still exist in a form that could be put to modern liturgical use. We can see the problem by looking at the medieval Latin liturgical terms that actually survive in modern English. From the cursus of the medieval Divine Office, for example, only the hour of None has become an ordinary English word: "noon." But in the process it has lost its technical meaning, unlike Vespers, Evensong, or Compline, which remain

---

[124] D. H. Green, *Language and History in the Early Germanic World* (Cambridge: Cambridge University Press 1998) 273–307, 341–73; note particularly the discussion of terms for Easter on pp. 351–54. Anna Helene Feulner, *Die griechische Lehnwörter im Altenglischen*, Münchener Universitäts-Schriften 21 (Frankfurt am Main: Peter Lang 2000) discusses a lot of religious terminology which, though ultimately of Greek origin, came into English from Latin.

[125] Throughout this article, my remarks on the history of English words are based on the documentation published in *The Oxford English Dictionary* [=OED], 2nd ed., ed. J. A. Simpson and E.S.C. Weiner (Oxford: Clarendon Press 1989), or the fuller documentation published in the *Middle English Dictionary* [=MED], ed. Hans Kurath et al. (Ann Arbor, Michigan: University of Michigan Press 1956–).

[126] Jacob Grimm and Wilhelm Grimm, *Deutsches Wörterbuch*, ed. Alfred Götze et al. 14/1.1 (Leipzig: S. Hirzel 1955) 707–14. The Roman blessing of the paschal candle uses the similar expression *vere beata nox* ("truly blessed night"), but of course it is speaking of Easter night, not Christmas night.

the names of religious services. None, of course, was the service held at the ninth hour of daylight, about 3 p.m. But because, on many days, it was only after None that monks finally got to eat, the service understandably crept backward to the time of day properly belonging to Sext, celebrated at the sixth hour of daylight or 12 o'clock. The meaning of "noon" in modern English, therefore, is not "the service of the ninth hour," but rather "lunchtime." Should we rename Daytime Prayer as "Noon Prayer" to pick up on this charming bit of language history, the result would not be a meaningful re-connection with the Roman liturgical tradition, but only an etymological absurdity.

There are many other examples of the trivializing capacity of etymological change, which some linguists call "verbicide."[127] In modern English "credo" can mean any core belief, "litany" any repetitive list (like a litany of complaints), and "mea culpa" little more than "sorry, my mistake!" "Requiem" can mean "eulogy," as when some newspaper pundit might editorialize a "Requiem for the Bull Market" or something. "Dirge" hardly reminds anyone of the Office of the Dead, where Matins began with the antiphon Dirige Domine — and no one who uses the word "placebo" thinks of the Vespers antiphon Placebo. In any case, since liturgical renewal, the Catholic funeral is a dirge no longer — a cynic might say that replacing the Dies irae with all that talk of resurrection has transformed it from dirge to placebo!

Popular expressions that retain some connotation of their liturgical origin tend to come, not from the Roman rite, but from the Book of Common Prayer — that is, from the historically dominant tradition of vernacular worship: "ashes to ashes," "chapter and verse," "to have and to hold," "speak now or forever hold his peace." The phrase "bell, book and candle," a reference to the excommunication ceremony, comes from Shakespeare (King John III.3.12). Nor is it necessarily the best theology that liturgical terms bring with them as they work their way through the language, if we can credit the seventeenth-century speculation that the incantation "hocus pocus" derives from Hoc est enim corpus meum ("for

---

[127] C. S. Lewis, Studies in Words (Cambridge: Cambridge University Press 1960, repr. 1996) 7–8, 131–32, 327–28. Geoffrey Hughes, Words in Time: A Social History of the English Vocabulary (Oxford: Basil Blackwell 1988) 14.

this is my body").[128] While there may be some anti-Catholic bias in the last example, in general the semantic weakening of liturgical and theological terms in colloquial speech is not caused by insufficient catechesis, misguided inculturation, or deliberate rejection of church teaching. It is, rather, an inevitable corollary of the statistical phenomenon known as "Zipf's Law": the more frequently a word is used, the more its original impact weakens into blandness. For the coffee-table linguists among us, the more jocular formulation is "Gresham's law of semantic change: Bad meanings drive out good."[129]

On the other hand, a word's popular meaning can preserve aspects of liturgical history that many would rather forget. "Legenda" in Latin literally means "something that is to be read." In the liturgy it was applied to the lives of the saints, which were read at the second nocturn of Matins. Thus the word understandably came to be used even of non-liturgical hagiographical texts that were studied in private, like the *Golden Legend*.[130] Since saints' lives were among the most popular materials for devotional reading in the vernacular, the word "legend" naturally passed into English. But the preposterous tall tales that characterized many of these stories gave rise to what is now the ordinary English meaning: a traditional, undocumented story that defies credibility, like the one about the departed co-worker whose coffee breaks were legendary. Few would want to revive this word for the modern Office of Readings, particularly when such a determined effort has been made to excise fictional texts from the Liturgy of the Hours — and the likes of St Christopher from the Calendar. The modern world finds plenty to ridicule in Christianity as it is, without our giving cause to revive the old monastic quip, "He can lie like a second nocturn!"

---

[128] *OED* 7:281-2.

[129] R. L. Trask, *Historical Linguistics* (London: Arnold 1996) 45. See also: H. Guiter and M. V. Arapov, eds., *Studies on Zipf's Law*, Quantitative Linguistics 16 (Bochum: Studienverlag Dr. N. Brockmeyer 1982); R. Harald Baayen, *Word Frequency Distributions*, Text, Speech and Language Technology 18 (Dordrecht: Kluwer Academic Publishers 2001).

[130] Jacobus de Voragine, *The Golden Legend: Readings on the Saints*, trans. William Granger Ryan (Princeton: Princeton University Press 1993).

The three issues of stratification, contact, and change intersect in the history of the word "lewd," which originally meant "lay": a lewd frere was a lay brother, for instance. It is not known whether the word originally derived from Latin "laicus," or from some Saxon or Romance term. Since Latin literacy was the most defining characteristic of the clerical part of society, "lewd" could also mean "illiterate" and even "ignorant" — this definition apparently included people who could read and write English, and were only illiterate in Latin. From there the word took on other connotations of coarseness and rudeness that the clergy (not without justification) ascribed to the laity — hence the word's modern meaning. But the loss of the original meaning tells us something too — that one of the forces driving language change is social change. We no longer live in a world where lay status implies lack of learning, where ecclesiastical education is the only or dominant kind, and the institutional church the major civilizing force in society. In the United States today, where many institutions of learning have given up their church affiliations, a sizable portion of at least the English-speaking laity is better educated than the average priest. Though the challenge of liturgical renewal has often been described as the restoration of some ancient ideal of universal participation, it would be more accurate historically to consider it an unprecedented effort to develop a worship for a new world, in which near-universal access to schooling has made most people capable of taking a more active role than was ever possible before in the history of the church.[131]

THE CLASSICS?

Only when we can deal with the threefold problem of language stratification, language contact, and language change can we respond knowledgeably to LA's advice: "works that are commonly considered 'classics' in a given vernacular language may prove useful in providing a suitable standard for its vocabulary and

[131] Even in the first century, "the written culture of antiquity was in the main restricted to a privileged minority," see William V. Harris, *Ancient Literacy* (Cambridge, Mass.: Harvard University Press 1989) 337. While literacy is obviously not essential to liturgical participation, it does enable more variety, more diversity of roles, and of course a greater emphasis on verbal/textual communication and interaction.

usage" (32). So where do we turn for models of sacral vernacular, in an English language blessed with hundreds of classics, from *The Dream of the Rood* to *Ulysses?*

" 'Read them,' said the King. The White Rabbit put on his spectacles. 'Where shall I begin, please your Majesty?' he asked. 'Begin at the beginning,' the King said, very gravely. . . .''[132]

In the beginning, language was poetry, and poetry was song. When ancient Anglo-Saxons gathered on winter evenings to pass a harp around, they sang long epics of heroic warriors — an oral literature we now know mainly from Beowulf, the earliest European vernacular epic and the only major Old English one that has been preserved in writing. Even Beowulf survives in only one manuscript, which was nearly destroyed in an eighteenth-century fire. So when monks from Pope Gregory's own monastery arrived in England bringing Roman Christianity, the locals received it as Roman song — Gregorian chant. St Wilfrid of York, who devoted his life to promoting Roman Christianity in place of the Celtic monastic kind in which he had been raised, once defended himself by thundering: "Was I not the first to convert the entire nation of Northumbria in accord with the mind of the Apostolic See . . .? Did I not teach the manner of singing according to the practice of the primitive church, with two choirs singing in harmony and alternating the responsories and antiphons? And did I not establish the monastic way of life according to the rule of St Benedict the Abbot which no one had yet introduced here?"[133] One cultural response to this Roman song was vernacular song. Caedmon, an illiterate peasant who herded cows for the abbey of Whitby, had been accustomed to sneak away whenever the after-dinner harp was brought out, embarrassed that he knew no songs. Yet one night, sleeping in the cowshed, he was told in a dream to sing the biblical story of creation, which he knew from the oral teaching of the monks. The next morning he sang it for the amazed brothers, who brought him to the abbess St Hilda. She pronounced it all a

---

[132] Lewis Carroll [Charles L. Dodgson], *The Annotated Alice: Alice's Adventures in Wonderland and Through the Looking Glass*, ed. Martin Gardner (Avenel, New Jersey: Wings Books 1960, repr. 1993) 158.

[133] Clinton Albertson, *Anglo-Saxon Saints and Heroes* (New York: Fordham University Press 1967) 143.

miracle, and Caedmon is remembered ever since as "the Father of English poetry."

Much surviving Old English literature, therefore, focuses on the Latin songs of the liturgy. Generations of schoolboys learned Latin with the help of Anglo-Saxon glosses between the lines of the psalms, hymns, and canticles of the Divine Office.[134] Poems of the kind ascribed to Cynewulf retell the O antiphons of Advent in the language of Beowulf.[135] A collection of poems that modern scholars call "The Benedictine Office" embodies a poetic response to the psalms and antiphons of the hours of the day.[136] It is "no mere literal and academic crib for poor Latinists: rather, it amounts to an exposition of the fuller import of the elements of the liturgy. . . . [H]eavily formulaic, with measured pace and spacious phrases — [it] may well be intended by its manner of articulation to offer scope for semi-formal meditation upon the words of the hallowed texts. By its very structure it enhances the thematic extension of each Latin proposition into a more complex statement of doctrine and dogma; it offers homage to the sentiment of the Latin by adorning it in the colours of English poetic rhetoric; and it causes the mind and heart to dwell upon and contemplate the subject-matter, unfolding phrase by phrase."[137]

But it is important to understand that these are all solid works of Germanic poetry, with typically teutonic stressed-based rhythms

[134] Helmut Gneuss, *Hymnar und Hymnen im englischen Mittelalter: Studien zur Überlieferung, Glossierung und Überstetzung lateinischer Hymnen in England,* Buchreihe der Anglia, Zeitschrift für englische Philologie 12 (Tübingen: M. Niemeyer 1968); Michael Korhammer, *Die monastischen Cantica im Mittelalter und ihre altenglischen Interlinearversionen: Studien und Textausg.,* Münchener Universitäts-Schriften: Philosophische Fakultät 6 (Munich: W. Fink 1976); Philip Pulsiano, ed., *Old English Glossed Psalters: Psalms 1-50* (Toronto: University of Toronto Press 2001).

[135] Susan Rankin, "The Liturgical Background of the Old English Advent Lyrics: A Reappraisal," *Learning and Literature in Anglo-Saxon England: Studies Presented to Peter Clemoes on the Occasion of his Sixty-Fifth Birthday,* ed. Michael Lapidge and Helmut Gneuss (Cambridge: Cambridge University Press 1985) 317–40.

[136] James M. Ure, ed., *The Benedictine Office: an Old English Text,* Edinburgh University Publications: Language & Literature 11 (Edinburgh: Edinburgh University Press 1957).

[137] S.A.J. Bradley, ed. and trans., *Anglo-Saxon Poetry,* The Everyman Library (London: J. M. Dent; Rutland, Vermont: Charles E. Tuttle 1982, repr. 2000) 537–38.

and alliteration, not mimicry of biblical psalmodic parallelism or quantity-based Latin meters. The earliest English poems could hardly be more unlike the servile approach to translation that *LA* envisions. Even the Anglo-Saxon Martyrology, though written in prose, is not a simple translation of Latin originals, but an original work.[138] Unfortunately there is a lot we still do not understand about the liturgy with which these texts were interacting. Anglo-Saxonists who have tried have had to admit that "the study of the history of the liturgy and its texts is probably the most complex and least accessible of the humanistic disciplines," and for the Anglo-Saxon period even the "study of the liturgy itself is in a relatively disordered state."[139] After all, the number of liturgiologists who can read medieval vernaculars is even smaller than the number of literary historians who read liturgical scholarship.

After the Norman Conquest of 1066 the language shifted from Old to Middle English. With a French ruling class, an English underclass, and a Latin-speaking clergy, the country became almost trilingual and, by the fourteenth century, better documentation makes it easier for us to trace the effects of stratification and language change. Some of the most accessible evidence of the English encounter with the liturgical language comes to us, not from the priests and bishops in the top stratum, who were fully comfortable with Latin, nor from those at the bottom who knew no Latin at all, but from people on the border of the clerical subculture, who

[138] Because the author was a knowledgeable reader of many Latin sources, some have speculated that he may have written a Latin text that was subsequently translated into Anglo-Saxon. But only the Anglo-Saxon version exists now, and it seems to me difficult to explain why the Latin (if it ever existed) would have disappeared. See J. E. Cross, "On the library of the Old English martyrologist," *Learning and Literature in Anglo-Saxon England: Studies Presented to Peter Clemoes on the Occasion of his Sixty-Fifth Birthday*, ed. Michael Lapidge and Helmut Gneuss (Cambridge: Cambridge University Press 1985) 127–49. Günter Kotzor, "The Latin Tradition of Martyrologies and the *Old English Martyrology*," *Studies in Earlier Old English Prose*, ed. Paul E. Szarmach (Albany: State University of New York Press 1986) 301–33.

[139] Milton McC. Gatch, "Old English literature and the liturgy: problems and potential," *Anglo-Saxon England* 6 (Cambridge University Press 1977) 237–47, quotes from 238, 239. More recently, M. Bradford Bedingfield has stated that "The study of the Anglo-Saxon liturgy is just coming into its own," in his book *The Dramatic Liturgy of Anglo-Saxon England*, Anglo-Saxon Studies (Woodbridge, UK, and Rochester, N.Y.: The Boydell Press 2002) 1.

knew how to use Latin but were more at home in their native tongue. One of them would be William Langland, who seems to have remained all his life a married cleric in minor orders. His lengthy poem *The Vision of Piers Plowman* reveals a mind shaped by the clerical formation of those days. Trained in childhood "to ding upon David each day till evening,"[140] his paying job consisted largely of chanting the psalms of the Office. Thus he filled his one literary opus with Latin quotations from the psalms and antiphons of the liturgy, and other texts that were read in ecclesiastical schools.

Books for religious women are particularly revealing: In the Processional of the Nuns of Chester,[141] we can observe the efforts of English-speaking women to worship in Latin. The corpus of Middle English texts surrounding the Ancrene Riwle ("Rule for Anchoresses") of about 1200 preserves the spiritual teaching that some learned Augustinian canons wrote for women with a wide range of proficiency: some who could recite the Office in Latin and some who could not, as well as their servants who could not read any language at all.[142]

Medieval books of hours (many of which belonged to wealthy women) seem to show that the economically advantaged laity prayed in Latin.[143] Indeed the use of such prayer books for teaching basic literacy led to the twofold meaning of the word "primer." Geoffrey Chaucer, a courtier who had received the most advanced and cosmopolitan education available, is an example of a layman

---

[140] "dyngen upon David eche day til eve," (B text, Passus III, line 312) in William Langland, *The Vision of Piers Plowman: A Critical Edition of the B-Text*, ed. A. V. C. Schmidt, 2nd ed., The Everyman Library (London: J. M. Dent 1995) 50 (my modernization).

[141] Peter Jeffery, "Popular Culture on the Periphery of the Medieval Liturgy," *Worship* 55 (1981) 419–27, especially 426–27.

[142] For an introduction see Anne Savage and Nicholas Watson, translators, *Anchoritic Spirituality: Ancrene Wisse and Associated Works*, The Classics of Western Spirituality (Mahwah, N.J.: Paulist Press 1991). A recent study is Elizabeth Robertson, *Early English Prose and the Female Audience* (Knoxville: University of Tennessee Press 1990).

[143] Books of hours are usually studied for their art and iconography. The relationships of such art to the texts is explored in: Roger W. Wieck, ed., *Time Sanctified: The Book of Hours in Medieval Art and Life* (New York: George Braziller; Baltimore: Walters Art Gallery 1988).

at the high end of the literacy spectrum. Although it is easier to identify the influence of French and Italian secular literature on him than to pin down his literary debt to the liturgy, it is certainly clear that he knew Latin theological and hagiographical texts, as well as sermons and glossed psalms in English.[144]

One of the best places to witness the interaction of sacred and secular language, liturgical and vernacular religious life, is the repertory of medieval carols, songs that (at least originally) were sung during the line dance known as the *carole*. Carols had many social functions in late medieval England, though there is much about their creation and use that we do not understand. They seem to have been sung in connection with processions following Vespers and other liturgical services — thus they may have had some relationship to the caroles that the French clergy danced upon the great labyrinths at Chartres and other Gothic cathedrals.[145] But in England carols were also sung at civil processions and ceremonies, a function that persisted in the carols of "The Boar's Head." When danced by lay men and women (or boys and girls?), carols could incorporate amorous games that were survivals of some

[144] The Parson's Tale is a typical medieval sermon. The Prioress's Prologue is a glossed form of Psalm 8. Her tale and the Second Nun's Tale are stories of martyrs. Many other writings of Chaucer give evidence of his familiarity with Latin theological literature and aspects of clerical life and culture, see Beverly Boyd, *Chaucer and the Liturgy* (Philadelphia: Dorrance 1967) and Edward E. Foster and David H. Carey, *Chaucer's Church: A Dictionary of Religious Terms in Chaucer* (Aldershot, U.K., and Brookfield, Vermont: Ashgate 2002). Chaucer's relationship to the English, French, and Latin of his time is studied in detail in Christopher Cannon, *The Making of Chaucer's English: A Study of Words* (Cambridge: Cambridge University Press 1998). Cannon essentially finds that Chaucer was not the innovator later generations took him to be, that most of the words he used, whatever language they derive from, were in circulation before his time.

[145] Hugo Rahner, *Man at Play*, trans. Brian Battershaw and Edward Quinn (New York: Herder and Herder 1967) 83–86; Penelope B. R. Doob, "The Auxerre Labyrinth Dance," *The Myriad Faces of Dance: Proceedings of the Eighth Annual Conference, Society of Dance Scholars, University of New Mexico, Department of Theatre Arts, Dance Division, Fine Arts Center, 15–17 February 1985*, compiled by Christena Schlundt (distributed at the conference) 132–41 [there is a copy at the New York Public Library, Performing Arts Branch, Research Division, Dance Collection]; Penelope Reed Doob, *The Idea of the Labyrinth from Classical Antiquity through the Middle Ages* (Ithaca: Cornell University Press 1990) 123–28; Craig Wright, *The Maze and the Warrior: Symbols in Architecture, Theology, and Music* (Cambridge, Mass.: Harvard University Press 2001) 132–58.

pre-Christian fertility religion, as in the male and female archetypes celebrated in carols of "The Holly and The Ivy." Yet the Franciscans also promoted carols with Christian themes, as part of their mission of preaching and instruction.[146] Carols demonstrate how the sacred-secular divide was much more fluid in those days than it is among us, in direct contrast to our stereotypes about the Middle Ages. As a result, carols provide valuable material for studying the interactions of liturgy and culture: "Whatever the ultimate resolution of the long-standing scholarly controversy on its origins, the carol is clearly one of many late medieval examples of the marriage of high and low, learned and popular."[147] This being so I cannot explain why, though our own era has tried so relentlessly to elevate sentimental pop songs into an ideal of "pastoral music," there has been so little research on the roles that songs and dances have actually played in the history of lay and even clerical spirituality.

The following fifteenth-century Christmas carol, for example, should be a classic within Anglophone liturgiology, for it is lewd in every sense of the word. The fact that it is not well known shows how little scholarship there has been on the lay experience of worship. No music survives, but the text exhibits typical structural features: it begins with a chorus known as a *burden*, sung by the whole group after each stanza. The stanzas, to be sung by a soloist or a small group, are written in a rough equivalent of Short Meter or "Poulter's measure" (four iambic lines of 3, 3, 4, and 3 stresses), rhyming at the second and fourth lines, then followed by a short refrain consisting of the words "Kyrie eleison" (spelled as one word, in typical medieval practice). The words of the Kyrie frequently occur in the refrains of medieval secular songs, in many languages, suggesting derivation from the litanies that were often used to give the laity something to sing during the liturgy. In this particular carol the function of the Kyrie refrain is to cue the burden, which is also based on "Kyrie eleison." The burden

[146] David L. Jeffrey, *The Early English Lyric & Franciscan Spirituality* (Lincoln: University of Nebraska Press 1975); Siegfried Wenzel, *Preachers, Poets, and the Early English Lyric* (Princeton: Princeton University Press 1986).

[147] Patrick S. Diehl, *The Medieval European Religious Lyric: An Ars Poetica* (Berkeley and Los Angeles: University of California Press 1985) 244, with a basic bibliography on pp. 245–47.

introduces the two characters in the song. Jankyn, a randy cleric in minor orders, would have had an education and status similar to Langland's; he reads the epistle and sings the chants, including the Kyrie of the burden itself. The odd spelling of "eleison" as "aleyson" seems to be a punning attempt to tell us that the other character, the female narrator, is named Alison. Her homespun metaphors make clear that she is a simple homemaker, and thus probably illiterate.[148]

Evidently Jankyn and Alison both walk in the procession to Christmas Mass, where Alison notices Jankyn's voice. Jankyn sings the introit and of course the Kyrie, then reads the Epistle,[149] all contributing to Alison's upbeat holiday mood: she feels blessed. With the approach to the Sanctus, apparently, Alison contributes to the collection, thinking that she is paying for Jankyn's fine clothes. He, meanwhile, shows off his talent for ornamenting the melody, breaking it up into little notes in a way that reminds Allison of dicing vegetables for cooking. The little notes seem to bunch together in tight clusters she calls "knots," as we might speak of a knot of onlookers — Alison is impressed. At the Agnus Dei, for the kiss of peace, Jankyn brings out the pax board — a small icon with a handle on it — which is passed around for people to kiss. The reason for this custom — a substitute for people kissing each other directly — is made all too clear by what happens next.

> [burden:] "Kyrie," so "Kyrie,"
> Jankyn singeth merry,
> With "aleyson."

[148] Jankyn and Allison are clearly folklore characters; we encounter their names in other songs and stories of the time. Most obviously, Chaucer's Wife of Bath, who like her mother was named Allison, took as her fifth husband a young cleric half her age named Jankyn, whom she met at her fourth husband's funeral when she found herself admiring his fine legs and feet.

[149] Jankyn's reading of the epistle suggests he had attained the order of subdeacon, in which case he would have been obligated to celibacy. But his singing of the chants and passing the pax board were roles typically given to clergy who had not yet received the subdiaconate. Moreover, if he were the subdeacon, we would not expect him to be singing the Sanctus, for at that point it would have been his job to stand at the foot of the altar with his back to the people, holding the paten. Thus the odds are that he belongs to a lower order such as lector or acolyte.

As I went on Yule Day
    in our procession,
Knew I jolly Jankyn
    by his merry tone.
Kyrieleyson.

Jankyn began the Introit
    on the Yule Day,
And yet me thinketh it does me good,
    so merry did he say,
"Kyrieleyson."

Jankyn read th'Epistle
    full fair and full well,
And yet me thinketh it does me good,
    as ever have I sel [=blessing].
Kyrieleyson.

Jankyn at the Sanctus
    crackleth a merry note,
And yet me thinketh it does me good:
    I paid for his coat.
Kyrieleyson.

Jankyn crackleth notes,
    a hundred in a knot
And yet he hacketh them smaller
    than greens to the pot.
Kyrieleyson.

Jankyn at the Agnus
    beareth the paxboard;
He winked, but said naught,
    and on my foot he trod.
Kyrieleyson.

Benedicamus Domino:
    Christ from shame me shield;
Deo gracias thereto:
    alas, I go with child!
Kyrieleyson.[150]

---

[150] Richard Leighton Greene, ed., *The Early English Carols* (Oxford: Clarendon Press 1935) 309.

The last stanza shows that this is not really a religious song at all, but more probably one of those carols that accompanied amorous games. The pagan elements of the old fertility rite have completely disappeared, however, and been replaced with a parody of Christian worship. The story is offensive, of course, particularly as it is said to have occurred on the feast of the Nativity — just the sort of cultural pandemonium the French epistle farces were meant to upstage. But blasphemous and ribald humor is ubiquitous in medieval literature; one cannot investigate vernacular religious language without encountering it. Indeed the irreligious character of this song makes it all the more useful for our present purpose: because it has no ecclesiastical agenda, we need not fear that it represents some imagined liturgy unconnected to practical reality. For the humor (such as it was) to work, the liturgical setting had to be immediately recognizable as typical. Our impression that this is a realistic depiction can find some support in the fact that dancing caroles in the churchyard, and ogling clerics in church, were two activities medieval women were instructed to confess.[151] Thus we can take the setting of this carol, with some confidence, as a candid "snapshot" of a commonplace church scene, an obviously incomplete but realistic layperson's eye-view of a Mass. As a result, the final stanza puts us squarely amid several intersecting questions about the languages of medieval worship.

Like many medieval songs in vernacular languages, this carol ends by quoting the Benedicamus Domino ("Let us bless the Lord") and its reply, Deo gratias ("Thanks be to God)." This was the dismissal formula at the end of office hours and other services, including Masses on less important days; thus it would not be out of place in the kind of carol that would accompany processions after Vespers, when the clergy came out of the enclosed choir, into the nave where the people were. Coming at the end of a Christmas Mass, though, it is technically incorrect, for on major feasts, when the Gloria in excelsis was sung, the dismissal command at Mass was Ite missa est ("Go, this is the dismissal") not Benedicamus Domino. Ite rarely if ever occurs in vernacular songs, however, so perhaps the anonymous poet chose carol convention over liturgical rubric.

[151] Savage and Watson, *Anchoritic Spirituality*, 165; Christopher Page, *The Owl and the Nightingale: Musical Life and Ideas in France 1100–1300* (Berkeley and Los Angeles: University of California Press 1989) 110–33.

In any case, at just the moment when Alison is supposed to respond "Deo gratias," she realizes her predicament and begins to pray in earnest, crying out in her native tongue. It is not only English words that she uses, but English idiom. "Christ shield me" is a kind of stock phrase in Middle English prayer — just the sort of thing one would tend to identify as an element of "sacral vernacular." One scholar involved in cataloguing such "pious formulae" has found that they "are rooted in a shared devotional consciousness and associated with an institutional discourse of doctrine and devotion." This "institutional discourse," however, was not centered in the Latin liturgy, but in areas where church life was carried on in the vernacular: preaching, catechesis, hagiography and religious drama, the literature of personal prayer and devotion.[152] The "pious formulae" fit well in the context of English literature, but it is difficult to trace them back to liturgical Latin antecedents: in this case, for example, the use of the word "shield" as a verb does not occur in Latin, though it does in Germanic and Slavic languages. Had Alison's vocabulary for prayer been limited to Anglicized expressions from the Latin liturgy, she might have burst out "Lord have mercy" or "Kyrie eleison," or (if she could read) with a verse from the Psalms, such as "Adprehende arma et scutum, et exsurge in adiutorium mihi!" (Ps 34[35]:2). To quote the Psalms in English, however, she would have had to choose between a paraphrase in very un-Latin rhyming couplets:

> Grip weapons and shield of fight,
> And rise in help to me with might![153]

— or a prose text in which the words for "weapons" and "shield" were glossed allegorically as "might" and "virtue":

Take might and virtue, and arise in help to me![154]

---

[152] Roger Dalrymple, *Language and Piety in Middle English Romance* (Cambridge: D. S. Brewer 2000) 33–63.

[153] Gripe wapenes and schelde of fighte / And rise in helpe to me with mighte (34:2). C. Horstman, ed., *Yorkshire Writers: Richard Rolle of Hampole and his Followers* 2 (London: Swan Sonnenschein 1896) 164.

[154] "Take myght and uertu, & aryse in helpe to me." Karl D. Bülbring, ed., *The Earliest Complete English Prose Psalter together with Eleven Canticles and a Translation*

But neither litany nor psalm comes to Alison's lips in her time of need. Instead she spontaneously uses the kind of expression we find in stories of King Arthur's knights, marked by typically Germanic alliteration: "Christ, shield me from shame!"[155] In other words, she has access to a traditional Christian English that exists in parallel with the liturgical language, but is not simply derived from it.

One does not want to draw too sweeping a conclusion from a single example, particularly as there is much we do not know about how carols were created and used. But the repertory of English carols is one venue where we regularly find snippets of liturgical Latin juxtaposed with lively, often devout English. This curious coexistence, in a genre so little understood, contrasts starkly with *LA*'s glib certitudes about liturgical Latin shaping everyday speech. The carols show (at the least) that, even long ago, inculturation was not necessarily a lecture, with the church expounding in precise Latin and the natives taking careful notes in the local patois. It was a dialogue, even if between unequals, reminiscent of the bilingual dialogue of the trisagion. Our task is to learn how to listen to such dialogues, and this will be the subject of the final chapter.

---

of the Athanasian Creed 1, Early English Text Society, old series 97 (London: Kegan Paul, Trench, Trübner & Co. 1891) 39. Another psalter of the period includes more extensive glosses with a more literal translation: "Gripe wapyns and sheld: and rise in help til me." H. R. Bramley, ed. *The Psalter or Psalms of David and Certain Canticles with a Translation and Exposition in English by Richard Rolle of Hampole* (Oxford: Clarendon Press 1884) 122.

[155] See the quotations cited in *MED*, vol. *S–SL*, p. 648. A good alliterative parallel to add to these is Piers Plowman (B text, Passus X, 404-6): "God grant it fare not so by folk that the faith teacheth / Of holy Church, that harbor is and God's house to save / And shield us from shame therein, as Noah's ship did beasts." William Langland, *The Vision of Piers Plowman: A Critical Edition of the B-Text*, ed. A.V.C. Schmidt, 161–62 (my modernization).

Chapter Four

Human and Angelic Tongues

A SUITABLE STANDARD?

"Not a lecture but a dialogue" is how I described the historical contact between the Roman rite and each of the cultures that accepted it. But I could say the same of history itself. History's characters endlessly debated each other on every conceivable issue, except when things disintegrated into outright conflict, as they frequently did. When we actually read the classics of early English, therefore, we find those who knew the truths of the faith and the riches of Catholic tradition wondering as much as we do now about how to communicate them to the faithful — and disagreeing as much as we do over competing solutions. For example, both Old and Middle English preserve large corpora of texts that render portions of the Bible into the vernacular.[156] Studying them gives us a lively picture of how the literate clergy used preaching, prayerbooks and pictures, song and story and theater, to bring the Scriptures into the ken of "lewd" people. In these texts, Bible and liturgy are inextricably intertwined, so that even what are purportedly "translations" of the Bible are full of allusions to sacraments and sacramentals, the canonical hours, psalms and antiphons, homilies and lives of saints. In the vernacular, as in Latin, the Bible

---

[156] James H. Morey, *Book and Verse: A Guide to Middle English Biblical Literature* (Urbana: University of Illinois Press 2000). Minnie Cate Morrell, *A Manual of Old English Biblical Materials* (Knoxville: University of Tennessee Press 1965). See also Albert S. Cook, *Biblical Quotations in Old English Prose Writers, edited with the Vulgate and other Latin Originals* (London: Macmillan 1898) and *Biblical Quotations in Old English Prose Writers: Second Series* (New York: Charles Scribner's Sons 1903).

was a living voice, a lived prayer, not markings on a page for the eyes only. Since the clergy of those days learned the Bible by singing the Mass and Office every day, it seemed perfectly natural to retell its stories in ballads and sculptures and mystery plays, without clearly distinguishing text from commentary, literal from liturgical wording, Biblical characters from the saints of later centuries.

By the fourteenth century, however, the age of Langland and Chaucer, a range of approaches had grown up, with much disagreement about which was more legitimate. At one end of the spectrum were the mendicant orders of friars: Dominicans, Franciscans, Carmelites and Augustinians. With their special commitment to preaching and teaching the faithful, it was the friars who made the greatest use of commentary, paraphrase, versification, song, dance, and other popularizing techniques. For this they were much criticized and ridiculed by the more conventional Christians in the middle of the spectrum, particularly as the secular clergy grew to resent the Friars' proclivity for dominating theological faculties and attracting penitents away from their own pastors. Because the friars supported themselves by begging, they were often accused of trying to attract larger contributions by tailoring their preaching, and the penances they imposed, to whatever the market would bear.[157] Thus Langland's complaint, echoing Allison's remark about paying for Jankin's coat:

I found there friars, all the four orders,
preaching to the people for the profit of their belly [cf. Philippians 3:19].
[They] glossed the Gospel as they well pleased;
From coveting [fine] cloaks they construed it as they would.[158]

---

[157] Robert Swanson, "The 'Mendicant Problem' in the Later Middle Ages," *The Medieval Church: Universities, Heresy, and the Religious Life: Essays in Honour of Gordon Leff*, ed. Peter Biller and Barrie Dobson, Studies in Church History: Subsidia 11 (Woodbridge: Boydell 1999) 217–38.

[158] I fond there freris, alle the foure ordris, / Prechinge the peple for profit of here wombe: / Gloside the gospel as hem good likide; / For coueitise of copis construide it as thei wolde. C text, lines 55–58, see William Langland, *Piers Plowman: A Parallel-Text Edition of the A, B, C and Z Versions* 1: Text, ed. A.V. C. Schmidt (London and New York: Longman 1995) 8–9. For discussion see Penn R. Szittya,

The view that the friars' willingness to adjust the Biblical text was more opportunistic than pastoral is well-known today from Geoffrey Chaucer's satirical account in *The Summoner's Tale*, wherein a friar drops by the house of a sick layman, boasts of his evangelical poverty while greeting the man's wife with a not-so-holy kiss, then asks what's for lunch. He assures the layman he just happened to be in the parish that day:

> I have today been at your church at Mass,
> And said a sermon, after my simple wit,
> Not all after the text of Holy Writ,
> For it is hard for you, as I suppose,
> And therefore will I teach you all the gloss.
> Glossing is a glorious thing, certainly,
> For "the letter slayeth" as we clergy say [2 Corinthians 3:6].[159]

After much effort, the friar succeeds in extracting a donation from the sick man, which, however, turns out to be a fart. The rest of the tale is a complex satire of the friars' ideals, Pythagorean mathematics, exegetical typology, Pentecost iconography, and much else, as the characters engage in scholastic debate over how to divide this mighty wind equally among the thirteen brothers of the friar's monastery.[160]

Chaucer's lighthearted tone contrasts sharply with the mood at the other end of the spectrum, where the Lollards advocated

---

The Antifraternal Tradition in Medieval Literature (Princeton: Princeton University Press 1986) 53, 255.

[159] I have today been at youre chirche at messe, / And seyd a sermon after my symple wit, / Nat al after the text of holy writ, / For it is hard to yow I suppose, / And therfore wol I teche yow all the glose. / Glosyng is a glorious thyng certeyn, / For lettre sleeth so as we clerkes seyn. *The Summoner's Tale*, lines 1788–94, ed. John F. Plummer, *A Variorum Edition of The Works of Geoffrey Chaucer 2: The Canterbury Tales 7: The Summoner's Tale* (Norman and London: University of Oklahoma Press 1995) 128–30. For comment see: John Fleming, "The Anifraternalism of the *Summoner's Tale*," *Journal of English and Germanic Philology* 65 (1966) 688–700. Fleming, "Anticlerical Satire as Theological Essay: Chaucer's *Summoner's Tale*," *Thalia* 6/1:5-22. Szittya, *The Antifraternal Tradition* 231–46.

[160] For brief analysis and bibliography see Helen Cooper, *The Canterbury Tales*, Oxford Guides to Chaucer (Oxford: Oxford University Press 1989, corrected repr. 1992) 176–83.

Translating Tradition

severely literal translation. The Lollard opinion of the friars, as expressed by one unamused writer, wasted no time on flippancy: "They cut short God's word, and tatter it by their rhymes, [so] that the form that Christ gave it is hid by hypocrisy."[161] The first Lollard translation of the Bible, only partially preserved, followed the Latin Vulgate word for word, so slavishly as to be difficult to understand. This translation was therefore revised to be somewhat more idiomatic; in the prologue to the revised version, the translator explained that he was still proceeding one word at a time, but had meanwhile learned to consider the entire sentence also, so as to choose a word that fit the context.[162]

Lay access to sacred texts was in fact one of the central concerns of the Lollard movement,[163] and all modern Christians, including Catholics, have benefited from the fact that the Lollards pressed the issue of literal translation. But everyone also knows where this position took them: into rejecting the traditions that had grown up around the Bible in the context of the Roman liturgy, and ultimately rejecting the teaching authority of the Roman church itself. It was the paraphrasing friars who remained within the Roman fold, the no-nonsense literalists who left. In time, of course, Lollard objections became more considerable and widely shared,

[161] "For thei docken Goddis word, and tateren it bi ther rimes, that the fowrme that Crist gaf it is hidde by ypocrisie." Morey, *Book and Verse* 11–12. Because they faced burning at the stake, Lollard writers had a powerful incentive to remain anonymous.

[162] Morey, *Book and Verse* 1–7, 11–13, 19–20, 85. The principles of translation are described in the General Prologue to the Lollard Bible, chapters 14–15, published in Josiah Forshall and Frederic Madden, eds., *The Holy Bible containing the Old and New Testaments, with the Apocryphal Books, in the Earliest English Versions Made from the Latin Vulgate by John Wycliffe and his Followers*, 4 vols. (Oxford: Oxford University Press 1850) 1:53–60. The author of the prologue knew the literature of patristic exegesis and summarizes the Fathers' rules for interpretation, but emphasizes the primacy of the literal sense. Those who prefer not to deal with fourteenth-century English may peruse *The Wycliffe New Testament (1388): An Edition in Modern Spelling*, ed. W. R. Cooper (London: The British Library 2002) — however this edition does not include the General Prologue.

[163] Anne Hudson, "'Laicus litteratus': the paradox of Lollardy," *Heresy and Literacy, 1000–1530*, ed. Peter Biller and Anne Hudson (Cambridge: Cambridge University Press 1994) 222–36. See also Anne Hudson, *The Premature Reformation: Wycliffite Texts and Lollard History* (Oxford: Clarendon Press 1988) 228–77.

and by the sixteenth century the humanistic recovery of Greek and Hebrew learning, the invention of printing, and other factors made possible the great Reformation translations of the Bible, while the Catholic Church reaffirmed its position that Scripture cannot be interpreted outside of Tradition. The reaction among English-speaking Catholics spawned the Rheims-Douay translation of the Bible (New Testament published 1582, Old Testament 1609–1610). It closely followed the Latin Vulgate with such "excessive literalness" that its integrity as a work of English is debatable.[164] Even the translators themselves realized this:

"We are very precise and religious in following our copy, the old vulgar approved Latin: not only in sense, which we hope we always do, but sometime in the very words also and phrases, which may seem rudeness or ignorance to the vulgar reader, and to common English ears not yet acquainted therewith."[165]

Non-Catholic scholars, lacking an instinctive reverence for the Vulgate, have seen no virtue in this approach: "The translation is almost always stiff and awkward, and not unfrequently meaningless."[166] One can decide for oneself by reading the Psalms, where even the Latin was often obscure. David comes off as a drunken fathead: "Thou hast fatted my head with oyle: and my chalice inebriating how goodlie is it!" (Psalm 22[23]:5). Resort to the chalice inebriating may help explain the presence of incomprehensible verses like "Before your thornes did vnderstand the old briar: as liuing so in wrath he swalloweth them" (Psalm 57[58]:10). The Douay version does get credit for introducing some Latin-derived expressions into the King James Version of 1611,[167] but apart from

---

[164] Hugh Pope, *The Catholic Student's "Aids" to the Study of the Bible* 1: *The Old Testament (General)* (London: Burns Oates & Washbourne 1926) 263. For more detail see Brooke Foss Westcott, *A General View of the History of the English Bible*, 3rd ed., rev. William Aldis Wright (London: Macmillan 1905) 102–6, 245–55.

[165] " We are very precise and religious in following our copie, the old vulgar approved Latin: not only in sense, which we hope we alwaies doe, but sometime in the very wordes also and phrases, which may seeme to the vulgar reader and to common English ears not yet acquainted therewith, rudeness or ignorance." Quoted from Pope, *Catholic Student's "Aids"* 260.

[166] Frederic Kenyon, *Our Bible and the Ancient Manuscripts*, rev. A. W. Adams (New York: Harper 1958) 302.

[167] James G. Carleton, *The Part of Rheims in the Making of the English Bible* (Oxford: Clarendon Press 1902). Charles C. Butterworth, *The Literary Lineage of the*

that it did not have much recognizable impact on English style, and certainly did not contribute to the development of a sacral vernacular. For that we must turn to the King James version itself,[168] and to the Book of Common Prayer, the Psalter of which is not the King James Version, but is based on translations by Myles Coverdale.[169]

Of course Catholics could learn much here, and the first thing they could learn is this: If you're looking for examples of liturgical language influencing ordinary speech, they are much easier to find in contexts where people actually worshipped in their own language. But an informative exploration of this vast and complex topic is precluded by *LA*, since it warns us to "avoid a wording or style that the Catholic faithful would confuse with the manner of speech of non-Catholic ecclesial communities" (40). For English-speakers, I personally doubt that it would be possible to ignore history in this way.

"AND WITH YOUR SPIRIT"?

What we find in the classics, then, is not a model of noble, sacral, Latinate English, which would solve our problems if only we had the humility to emulate it. Instead we find that, centuries ago, people already disagreed about the same issue that the *LA* authors want to be disagreeable about today: even in very different historical and cultural contexts, people challenged and defended a range

---

King James Bible, 1340–1611 (Philadelphia: University of Pennsylvania Press 1941) 191–97, 202–5. F. F. Bruce, *The English Bible: A History of Translations from the earliest English Versions to the New English Bible,* rev. ed. (London: Lutterworth Press 1970) 113–26.

[168] On the other hand Ronald Knox, the last person to translate the Vulgate into English, argued in *The Trials of a Translator* (New York: Sheed & Ward 1949) p. 75, that "The Authorized Version is good English only because English writers, for centuries, have treated it as the standard of good English. In itself, it is no better English than the Douay."

[169] Coverdale did not know Hebrew, but worked from a Protestant translation into Latin, informed both by earlier English versions and by continental Protestant translations. The traditional Prayer Book Psalter, however, has a complex transmission history of its own, so that it does not conform exactly to any of Coverdale's publications. Stella Brook, *The Language of The Book of Common Prayer* (New York: Oxford University Press 1965) 148–71. Westcott, *A General View* 198–207. Butterworth, *Literary Lineage* 143–45, 153–57. A. C. Partridge, *English Biblical Translation* (London: André Deutsch 1973) 149–58.

Human and Angelic Tongues

of positions and opinions on how to use language. The question — to gloss or not to gloss — hasn't changed, and neither has the fact that there is more than one justifiable answer.

One can see the problem in a small way in the most common of liturgical answers, the one we give to "The Lord be with you." Responding "And with your spirit" (*LA* 56) keeps us closer to the Biblical originals (Galatians 6:18, 2 Timothy 4:22, Philemon 25, 2 Thessalonians 3:16, Ruth 2:4, etc.), opens up to us the rich language of Biblical greetings and the even richer theme of "spirit."[170] But many people, both laity and priests, will miss all these allusions. And where texts or practices are no longer understood, odd and misleading explanations, including non-Biblical concepts of "spirit," will arise almost spontaneously to fill the vacuum. "And also with you," on the other hand, lacks all pretense at poetry, and closes a door that some people, who have the potential to appreciate Biblical resonances, might otherwise have entered. But no one will have any doubt about what it means.[171]

If there is to be only one text that everyone must use, my personal preference would be for the more literal translation — better to give everyone the incentive to explore the deeper meaning than

---

[170] Michael K. Magee, "The Liturgical Translation of the Response "*Et Cum Spiritu Tuo*," *Communio* 29 (Spring 2002) 152–71.

[171] There are also those who say of "et cum spiritu tuo" that "these words are no more than a Semitic paraphrase of the simple 'And with you.'" This view was promoted, for example, in Ludwig Eisenhofer and Joseph Lechner, *The Liturgy of the Roman Rite*, trans. A. J. and E. F. Peeler, ed. H. E. Winstone (New York: Herder and Herder 1961) 76, following whom it was popularized through Joseph A. Jungmann, *The Mass of the Roman Rite: Its Origins and Development (Missarum Sollemnia)* 1, trans. Francis A. Brunner (New York: Benziger Brothers 1951) 363 note 16. It has recently been defended in Mary M. Schaefer, "Implementing *Liturgiam Authenticam*: A Response to Bruce Harbert," *Antiphon: A Journal for Liturgical Renewal* 7/1 (2002) 40–45, see 40. That Hebrew "spirit" can be a synonym for "soul" or "self" is clear enough, see *Theologisches Wörterbuch zum Alten Testament* 7, ed. Heinz-Josef Fabry and Helmer Ringgren et al. (Stuttgart: W. Kohlhammer 1993) 407–10. But surely the Christian liturgical expression derives in particular from the Pauline usage, in which "God's Spirit [though] never evaporating into the [spirit] given individually to man, is also the innermost ego of the one who no longer lives by his own being but by God's being for him." See *Theological Dictionary of the New Testament*, ed. Gerhard Friedrich, trans. Geoffrey W. Bromiley 6 (Grand Rapids, Michigan: Eerdmans 1968) 436. This sense is lost when "your spirit" is equated with "you."

Translating Tradition

to subject all of us to "dumbing down." But either approach can be justified. Who is it, after all, that comes to us in the Church's liturgy? The Christ who, being lifted up from the earth, draws all people to himself? Or the Jesus who empties himself, taking the form of a slave? Both, of course, for they are the same. What an awe-full task it is, then, to draw up a text that is open in both directions: "a river both wide and deep, in which a lamb can wade and an elephant swim."[172] What losses can result when Church leaders at any level press one model too far at the expense of the other, and how tragic when the translators who struggle so mightily with these issues are accused of harboring base motives and political agendas! Openness to diversity can be a way out of adversity and toward unity. A modern friar, then, might gloss the original Preacher by pointing out that there is a season for everything: a time to paraphrase (that is, to embrace), and a time to refrain from paraphrasing (Ecclesiastes 3:5).

If the issues haven't changed since Chaucer's day, what have changed are the absurdities. We now have the documents of Vatican II to show how balancing diverse ecclesiologies expresses the mystery of the Church more fully than any single model can.[173] Yet "real" life in today's church seems more like a standoff between conservatives who think they own the past and liberals determined to own the future. One group takes as its mantra a kind of apophatic ecclesiology of bumper-sticker bluntness: "The Church is not a democracy" — while the other retorts with picket-sign pugnacity that it's not a dictatorship either. I feel like raising my hand and asking, "What was the question, again?" And the absurdities pile up: The Vatican issues a statement urging the tradition of the Fathers, but cites not a single patristic writing. The Roman church appeals to its own belated attempt to undo centuries of Westernizing the Eastern rites, in order to justify "preserving" a "Roman rite" that is not the historic Roman rite. The Holy See advocates unprecedented literalism with near-Lollard ferocity, while Protestants who rightly claim the Lollard heritage look on aghast. Church officials too busy to enjoy English literature send

[172] Gregory, *Moralia in Job*, Epistula Leandro 4, CCL 143:6.
[173] As classically outlined in Avery Dulles, *Models of the Church*, expanded ed. (Garden City, N.Y.: Doubleday Image Books 1978).

Human and Angelic Tongues

us to our own classics in search of a worthy liturgical idiom, but we find only fart jokes so arcane that it took generations of medievalists from a raft of disciplines to locate the punch lines. Only now, in today's unhappy Church, we have no modern-day Chaucer to help us regain a healthy perspective.

But the divinely-ordained purpose of absurdity is to throw the truth into sharp relief, and the truth these absurdities bring out is that anyone who claims "history is on my side" will find it an unreliable ally. How cultures in the past adapted, or adapted to, the Roman rite is not something we all know that can be summed up in a few words, like an Aesopian fable with an inevitable and timeless moral. It is, instead, a subject of great complexity, of which I am only scratching the surface here. Even when the facts are better known, however, looking to the past for answers is like seeing a riddle in a mirror (1 Corinthians 13:12, Vulgate), for there are two sources of difficulty. The riddle is that history is not a straightforward narrative, but a great contest of ideals and forces, full of clashing and competing stances and positions, roads taken and not taken, experiments that failed but were imposed anyway, lucky gambles that succeeded but were stifled nonetheless, half-built structures converted to other purposes, problems a lot like our problems all twisted up with problems we can't imagine having, plenty of pain and suffering all around. The mirror is the distortions imposed by our own time-conditioned preconceptions, which prevent us from seeing the past as it actually was: changes in language, loss and dispersal of sources, idea systems that no longer come naturally, loyalties to causes and movements that didn't exist back then, or somehow did. The riddle, in short, is ourselves, the human race, and the mirror is time.

A NEW ERA?

Speaking of riddles in time, in a sense *LA* is already too late. Invoking a past its authors do not really remember, it promises — or threatens — a future that Yogi Berra might have called "déjà vu like you never saw before." Even the Vatican II terminology ("inculturation," "authentic renewal," "pastoral necessity") seems so disconnected from its sources in the Conciliar documents that I can see why *LA* looks to some people (though I disagree with them) like a cynical attempt to manipulate whatever buzzwords it will

Translating Tradition

take to curb gender-inclusive language — a dog so bad, it seems, that any stick is good enough to beat it with.

But if historical knowledge of the Roman tradition has evaporated this completely, then the kind of "Tridentine" restoration some people fear is no longer possible. On the basis of documents like *LA*, we could never bring back the Counter-Reformation church, with its glorious choir of paddle-wielding schoolteachers, its admirable company of liturgical rubricists, its white-robed host of moralizing probabiliorists, terrible as an army with banners. But we could erect a cruel caricature of it, vastly more impoverished and repressive than the original ever was. There are none-too-subtle indications that that is just what *LA*'s talk of a "new era" really means.

"The readiness to see one's own work examined and revised by others is an essential trait" for those working with liturgical texts, *LA* warns us (75). Who can deny it? The work requires, as *LA* says, both a "spirit of prayer" and "a rare degree of expertise." The need for expertise is self-evident: the Christian liturgical tradition is as long as history, as wide as humanity, as complex as civilization. Nobody could ever know it all. But if the *LA* authors perceive a need to emphasize this, here is one more historical development they are unaware of: These days, anyone who has the scholarly competence to translate a liturgy is already accustomed to seeing her work examined, criticized, and improved by others. It is built into the academic workplace in a dozen ways, through the use of respondents and panel formats at conferences, peer review, promotion review, book reviews, review articles, and so on. Every year I am consulted by publishers, editors, universities, granting-making entities, and international cultural agencies for my opinion on other people's work, and others are asked to judge mine by identical standards. Liturgical scholars and translators are not afraid to have their work reviewed by Church authorities. What we fear is having it "revised" by people who invoke Church Fathers they haven't read, whose theories of language and culture were created *ex nihilo*, who cannot tell the New Vulgate from the old one.

But the most worrisome thing about *LA* is that what it lacks in factuality it makes up with naked aggression. It speaks words of power and control rather than cooperation and consultation, much less charity. Asserting a right to impose translations on episcopal conferences (104), or take charge of any translation that might be used in Rome itself (76) are the kind of thing I mean, and the latest news is that a new translation is already in preparation. No less scary is the stipulation that everyone involved in liturgical translation, "including the experts," are to be bound to confidentiality by contract (101). This will certainly insulate them from political pressure groups bent on twisting the translations, if there are any. But it will also insulate them from everyone else, including many people who, though not under contract, could have been helpful with Biblical language, theological terminology, the linguistics of the vernacular, as well what is "suitable for being set to music" (60). The translators and experts are, after all, performing a public service to the whole church, not a private service to the bishops or the Vatican. Of course there is a role for confidentiality; like many academics I, too, have written confidential reports for international non-governmental organizations. But the purpose of confidentiality is to protect the vulnerable from being harmed by disclosures of sensitive information. This includes the expert, who is freed to be more objective by being shielded from any repercussions her advice might provoke. It is an abuse of confidentiality to use it to isolate the expert and control the content of her advice, indeed it renders superfluous the whole notion of "expertise."

To read the sources of the Catholic tradition is to learn that, *contrariis quibuslibet minime obstantibus*, the language of intimidation and domination is not our native tongue. The first pope, for instance, was remembered as having taught presbyters to "tend the flock of God . . ., not by constraint but willingly. . . . Do not lord it over those assigned to you, but be examples to the flock" (1 Peter 5:1-3). It is particularly embarrassing that all this muscular Christianity comes to us vested and mitred in the most ignorant statement on liturgy ever issued by a modern Vatican congregation. But in a millennium when a Pope can apologize to the Jews, it is not too much to hope that the Dicastery, too, will find the courage to lead by example, and practice what it preaches on the matter of accepting correction. It should not have to be one more reason why translators will need a spirit of prayer.

Anselm of Laon (ca. 1050-1117), a great teacher of the first generation of Scholastics (not to be confused with the more famous St Anselm of Canterbury), wrote this to an abbot who had consulted him about a difficult passage in the Church Fathers:

"It seems that the controversy that is so stirred up among you is not about the passage [sententia], but about quarrels over words. It is adult to discuss correct meanings [sensus], but to dispute about words is for children, who little understand what they say or hear. The Apostle reproves them, 'Do not be childish in your thinking [sensibus];' instead he teaches, 'Be childlike with respect to evil' [1 Corinthians 14:20]. Some people do not pay attention to these things, because they are completely puffed up with nominal learning and do not know the meaning [sensus] of the Fathers. As the Apostle says, 'they have a weakness for controversies and quarrels over words' [1 Timothy 6:4]. However the statements [sententiae] of all the Catholic Fathers are diverse, but not adverse; they concur by 'coming together as one' [1 Corinthians 14:23]. It is true that certain contrarieties, as it were, and quarrels resonate in the words, as a result of which the petty are scandalized, the restless are disturbed, the proud contend, and the truly knowledgeable are excluded, though they could easily show the others that the dissonance harmonizes.

"On the subject of 'quarrels about words,' these things are put forth in the Scriptures: 'The Lord does not want evil. . . .' [other similar quotations follow]."[174]

It may have been Anselm who first applied the "diverse but not adverse" formulation to the study of Catholic tradition — it already had seen long use in Biblical exegesis. He apparently said it often, for the principle echoes throughout Scholastic thinking, in eloquent testimony to the influence of a man who was known as "the teacher of teachers."[175] In our time, when the imposing Aristotelian structure of Scholasticism is often perceived as diametrically opposed to all that Vatican II allegedly represents, it is helpful to remember that even Scholasticism began with Anselm's good sense of proportion, his appreciation of diversity, and his unwavering confidence that, for the "truly knowledgeable . . . the dissonance harmonizes."

[174] PL 162:1587.
[175] J. De Ghellinck, *Le mouvement théologique du XIIe siècle: Études, recherches et documents*, 2nd ed. (Bruges: De Tempel 1948) 517–23, see also 133–48. Henri de Lubac, "À propos de la formule: 'Diversi, sed non adversi,'" *Mélanges Jules Lebreton* 2, Recherches de science religieuse 40 (Paris: Bureaux de la Revue 1952) 27–40.

The dissonant quarrels of today resonate in just the kind of mistrust between theologians and church leaders that is so evident in *LA*. But the way toward harmonizing this discord is pointed out by Vatican II itself. One of the most important developments at the Council, in my opinion, was its move beyond the conventional "two-source theory" of revelation, to a new insight that "sacred tradition, sacred Scripture, and the magisterium of the church . . . are so connected and associated that one of them does not stand without the others."[176] Without tradition, we cannot interpret Scripture. Without Church teaching, we cannot distinguish authentic tradition from mere historical precedent. But it seems to me this must also mean that the magisterium cannot teach in isolation from Scripture and tradition; those who exercise the teaching ministry bear a grave responsibility to ensure that what they say is rooted in both. That is why it is essential that those who formulate church teachings and policies maintain good working relationships with scholars who, though lacking the apostolic teaching mandate, are widely and deeply informed about the content of Scripture and tradition. Ordination and ecclesiastical appointment do not imbue a person with knowledge of how the liturgy grew and developed over time, any more than the knowledge of ancient languages and texts empowers anyone to teach in the name of the Church. Both those who teach and those who know, therefore, must do all they can to keep the lines of communication open so that they can perennially listen to each other. Oaths of secrecy, tendentious misrepresentations of tradition, exercises of raw power are not the life to which we are called. "Let everyone be quick to listen, slow to speak, slow to anger, for the wrath of man does not accomplish the righteousness of God" (James 1:19-20). It is not the absence of conflict that makes the Church different from other communities — the New Testament is full of stories about conflicts between Christians. What makes Christians different is, or should be, how we handle the conflicts that inevitably arise.

CAN THE ROMAN RITE BE SAVED?

Liturgiam Authenticam should be summarily withdrawn, on the grounds that it was released prematurely, before proper consulta-

---

[176] *Dei Verbum* 10, trans. Tanner, *Decrees* 2:975 (modified).

Translating Tradition

tion with a sufficient number of experts had been completed. Then only the hard part will remain: what to do about the issues and tensions that produced it. "Let everyone be quick to listen": Careful and charitable listening to what our fellow Christians are trying to say should always be the first step. Why do some people want a more formal kind of language that looks back to literary classics and to Latin?

Archaism. In a classic work of literary criticism, Owen Barfield argued that there is an essential relationship between archaic language and poetic language, rooted in the way language naturally develops over time. "The natural progress of language, if left, as it were, to itself, is a progress from poetic towards prosaic . . .,"[177] he wrote. In this he was following Ralph Waldo Emerson, who a century earlier had written that words began as metaphoric descriptions of phenomena encountered in the world of nature.

"As we go back in history, language becomes more picturesque, until its infancy, when it is all poetry; or, all spiritual facts are represented by natural symbols. . . . And as this is the first language, so is it the last. This immediate dependence of language upon nature . . . never loses its power to affect us."[178]

Poetry, as Barfield saw it, seeks to reverse the process, as if re-imagining a time when the same word could mean "wind," "breath," and "spirit," all three, as in John 3:8.

"'The language of the age', wrote [Thomas] Gray, 'is never the language of poetry. . . .' Indeed, to the average person, the phrase 'poetic diction' is probably almost synonymous with what the literary mean by 'Archaism'."[179]

[177] Owen Barfield, *Poetic Diction: A Study in Meaning*, [3rd ed.] (Middletown, Conn.: Wesleyan University Press 1984) 152.

[178] Ralph Waldo Emerson, *Nature* (Boston: James Munroe 1836) 37; reprinted with contemporary and later criticism in Merton M. Sealts and Alfred R. Ferguson, eds., *Emerson's Nature — Origin, Growth, Meaning* (New York: Dodd, Mead 1969) see p. 16. The passage is quoted in Barfield, *Poetic Diction* p. 92.

[179] Barfield, *Poetic Diction* 152–53, see also 158 on inauthentic archaism. On the quote from Thomas Gray see Richard Terry, "Gray and Poetic Diction" in *Thomas Gray: Contemporary Essays*, ed. W. B. Hutchings and William Ruddick (Liverpool University Press 1993) 73–110, especially 79–80.

We have already seen examples of the "progress from poetic towards prosaic," in our earlier examples of "verbicide:" the trajectory from None to noon, from the legendae of the saints to mere legend. The etymology of "placebo" exemplifies this process well: To begin with, Vulgate Psalm 114 (=NAB 116:1-9) was appropriately chosen to begin Vespers for the Dead. Then its final verse supplied the antiphon Placebo domino, "I will be welcome/pleasing to the Lord in the land of the living." As the opening word of the first antiphon, Placebo became a shorthand term for the entire Vespers, even the entire Office of the Dead, just as the word Requiem did for the Mass of the Dead. With the development of the late-medieval patronage system, low-level clergy earned subsistence wages chanting the Office of the Dead in the private chapels of aristocratic families; so the verse acquired a sarcastic connotation of pleasing an earthly lord in order to remain among the living. "Singing placebo" then became a slang expression for flattery, an essential survival skill in a patronage economy. As Europe evolved toward a mercantile economy, sucking up to dukes was replaced by giving customers what they want, and we end up with a sugar pill.

Since Barfield, of course, any number of modern poets have demonstrated that it is perfectly possible to write poetry in "the language of the age," just as any number of post-modern critics have demonstrated that it is possible to write theories of literature more impenetrable than any poetry. So let us think, instead, of archaic language as a register or style, one of many choices available in a poet's creative palette. It wasn't the Beats' weapon of choice (and they were the best minds of my generation!), but it could be important to the poet who seeks, like William Blake

> To see a World in a Grain of Sand
> And a Heaven in a Wild Flower,
> Hold Infinity in the palm of your hand,
> And Eternity in an hour.

To that sort of poet, restricting the word "man" to the definition "adult male" may feel like trading away the semantically wide and historically deep field of meanings and connotations that the word has traditionally carried, in exchange for a cheap, polarizing political element that threatens the cohesion or even the survival of the community. As Blake says later in the same poem,

The Winner's Shout, the Loser's Curse,
Dance before dead England's Hearse.[180]

Of course there are other sides to the gendered-language issue; some would disagree as to where the polarization is really coming from. But for the moment let us keep listening.

"I find that people re-act to archaism most diversely," wrote C. S. Lewis, a professional historian of the English language. "It antagonises some: makes what is said unreal. To others, not necessarily more learned, it is highly numinous and a real aid to devotion. We can't please both."[181] But in a worldwide church, we must provide pastoral care to both. We can't simply tell *LA* supporters that all the delusions will go away if they will just keep fingersnapping to "They'll know we are Christians" till they can feel the groove. Instead, all of us must work to construct a more inclusive liturgy, informed by the full spectrum of traditional models and human experience, each of us taking care not to wound the weak conscience of our brother, for whom Christ died (1 Corinthians 8:10-13).

It is not by chance that archaic, formal, classical language is common in the human experience of worship, Christian and non-Christian. Since we live within the bounds of time, the experience of doing and saying ancient, ancestral things can be a powerful metaphor for eternity, a way to connect with emotions and desires so basic that they feel primeval. In the Christian tradition, deliberately archaic language is as old as the Bible — for example in Luke's use of Septuagint Greek though he was capable of a more

---

[180] "Auguries of Innocence" in David V. Erdman, ed., *The Complete Poetry and Prose of William Blake*, newly rev. ed. (Berkeley and Los Angeles: University of California Press 1982) 490, 492, my punctuation.

[181] C. S. Lewis, *Letters to Malcolm: Chiefly on Prayer* (London: Geoffrey Bles 1964) 16. It is worth reading Lewis's complete remarks on liturgical vernacular in this book; his critique of "timeless English" (p. 14) may be a reply to Knox, *Trials of a Translator* p. 19. Other essays by Lewis on the subject include "Miserable Offenders: An Interpretation of Prayer Book Language" and "Modern Translations of the Bible," in C. S. Lewis, *Essay Collection and Other Short Pieces*, ed. Lesley Walmsley (London: Harper Collins 2000) 461–65, 472–75.

classical style,[182] in the (also very Lucan) tendency to associate prophecy with poetry,[183] in the many recountings of larger-than-life salvific events as "mysteries of the past, things hidden from the foundation of the world" (cf. Psalm 78:2, Matthew 13:35) that make our modern-educated children ask, "Did that really happen?" Indeed, anyone who thinks archaic "Bible English" cannot possibly be meaningful to modern people of limited education and social status should visit an urban storefront church[184] — or listen to reggae music, in which the vocabulary and phrasing of the King James Bible shape the rebellious Rastafarian rhetoric of one of the most oppressed populations on the planet.[185]

Thus modern people who deliberately invoke the archaic are not necessarily being dishonest, insincere or "phony." They can also be seen as employing a kind of poetry, indeed a very accessible kind, which appears in a range of pop-culture guises besides reggae. For instance, the imagined mythical "past" of fantasy science fiction, from *The Lord of the Rings* to *Star Wars*, evokes a pseudo-medieval world of quests and crusades, of sword-fighting warriors battling fantastic creatures over lost kingdoms long ago. Real medievalists may scruple (though the author of *The Lord of the Rings* was a real medievalist) but devotees know that what they are enjoying was created in the twentieth century. They nonetheless find such fic-

---

[182] Joseph A. Fitzmyer, *The Gospel According to Luke (I–IX)*, The Anchor Bible (New York: Doubleday 1981) 113–16.

[183] David Noel Freedman, *Pottery, Poetry, and Prophecy: Studies in Early Hebrew Poetry* (Winona Lake, Indiana: Eisenbrauns 1980) 1–22.

[184] Gerald L. Davis, *I got the Word in me and I can sing it, you know: A Study of the Performed African-American Sermon* (Philadelphia: University of Pennsylvania Press 1985) especially 115–51.

[185] Ken Post, "The Bible as Ideology: Ethiopianism in Jamaica, 1930–38," *African Perspectives: Papers in the History, Politics and Economics of Africa presented to Thomas Hodgkin*, ed. Christopher Allen and R. W. Johnson (Cambridge: Cambridge University Press 1970) 185–207. Michael Jackson, "Rastafarianism," *Theology* 83 (1980) 26–34. Laurence A. Breiner, "The English Bible in Jamaican Rastafarianism," *Journal of Religious Thought* 42/2 (1985–86) 30–43. Nathaniel Samuel Murrell and Lewin Williams, "The Black Biblical Hermeneutics of Rastafari," *Chanting Down Babylon: The Rastafari Reader*, ed. Nathaniel Samuel Murrell et al. (Philadelphia: Temple University Press 1998) 326–48. In July of 2003, an extensive catalogue of Biblical allusions in reggae lyrics was available at the very informative Words of Wisdom web site, homepage.ntlworld.com/davebulow/wow/index.htm.

tional pasts a compelling way to deal with timeless issues of good and evil, identity and commitment. Worship presented as archaic can nurture a strong feeling of wholeness, an atavistic sense of oneness between past and present, between natural and divine. "Not invariance itself, but apparent invariance," what a scholar would consider a fictive enactment of invariance, can compellingly express "ever-unvarying-eternal-messages."[186] Some Christians who do not find this experience in contemporary worship will turn elsewhere; hence the appeal of things like Transcendental Meditation — techniques for suspending the mind's sense of time and space — whose proponents regularly espouse creation myths that would make the meditation experience the essence and origin of all religions.[187] Other Christians feel drawn to pre-Conciliar models of liturgy.

As I interpret *LA*, therefore, its main motivation is not opposition to inclusive language as such — that is only a symptom of what its authors really want. What they really want is a more profound sense of the sacred, an experience of connection to what seems age-old and eternal, uniting past and present in an unchanging rite that is above the ebb and flow of ordinary history. That is why they imagine the current Roman rite as the virtually unchanged tradition of the Fathers, which liturgical renewal only burnished even more brightly. The historically informed know better, but handing out bibliographies will not fill the deep need felt by many people (even many young people) for a sense of oneness and sacrality that they cannot find in the liturgies actually taking place in churches today. It is time to accept that this desire of theirs is not an intrinsically bad thing, but a common human need even though not a universal one. It is unjust to denigrate it as mere nostalgia or ignorance, even in the not-uncommon situations where nostalgia and ignorance are palpably present — for something precious really has been misplaced, and the demand for

---

[186] Roy A. Rappaport, *Ritual and Religion in the Making of Humanity* (Cambridge University Press 1999) 444.

[187] One expression of this myth, couched in the vocabulary of modern science, is Andrew Newberg, Eugene d'Aquili and Vince Rause, *Why God Won't Go Away: Brain Science and the Biology of Belief* (New York: Ballantine Books 2001). The authors would have been well-advised to have at least one conversation with an expert in comparative religion.

Human and Angelic Tongues

more reverence at worship is some people's way of asking for it back. Let us acknowledge that, over the course of history, the same Catholic tradition that revels in a diversity of rites has also put forward more than one ideal of Christian worship, and there is no a priori reason why current practice cannot honor all of them. It is only a question of how.

Two Liturgical Ideals. Now that we have listened, therefore, the second step is to review and reconsider the tradition in its fullness. Liturgical history reveals many ways to nurture experiences of the holy — some that employ language, others that use non-verbal media. We have already seen that the traditional texts of the Roman rite had at least two important ways to express a unity across time and space: allegorical exegesis and hagiological typology. Both involve a highly metaphoric use of language, expressing a deeper mystery in terms of a lesser one: The story of Jeremiah's persecution, retold on the spot of John's persecution, refracts a binocular, three-dimensional image of the Just One who was despised and rejected for the sake of us all. Metaphor of this kind hardly seems out of place in a rite wherein a cup of wine becomes the blood of an innocent murder victim, through whom the creator of the world saves his people from death. This spirit governed the Roman tradition of celebrating the Eucharist for centuries, summed up in the following highly influential description by Pope Gregory the Great:

"Indeed, this sacrificial victim saves the soul from eternal destruction in a singular way, for by a mystery it brings back for us that death of the only-begotten one who, though 'rising from the dead he now dies no more, and death has power over him no longer' (Romans 6:9), and though living immortally and incorruptibly from his own self, is immolated again for us in this mystery of the sacred oblation. There his body is surely eaten, his flesh is distributed for the health of the people, his blood is poured out — not now into the hands of unbelievers, but into the mouths of the faithful. Therefore let us consider what kind of sacrifice this is for us, which always re-presents, for our absolution, the passion of the only-begotten Son. For who among the faithful can doubt that, in this moment of immolation, at the voice of the priest, the heavens are opened, the choirs of angels draw near in that mystery of Jesus Christ, the lowest things are united to the highest, earthly things are joined to heavenly, and from visible and invisible things a oneness comes into being?"[188]

Gregory's reputation as one of the main architects of the Roman sacramentary contributed, of course, to the influence of this passage, which eventually found visual expression in the icono-graphical theme known as "The Mass of St Gregory."[189] We might call this a "Gregorian" model of the Eucharist, to distinguish it from other possible models.

The heavens opening, choirs of angels, earthly and heavenly things brought together in a unity of seen and unseen — that is what people were taught for generations to expect at the Roman Mass, at the central moment when "the words of the priest" re-peated the eucharistic words of Jesus. For many Catholics it meant that, for a brief time during each busy week, they were privileged, like Blake's poet, to "hold Infinity in the palm of your hand" (or at least on the tip of the tongue!) "and Eternity in an hour" (cf. Matthew 26:40). The medieval preaching that one did not grow older during the brief moments of gazing at the elevated host[190] expressed this in yet another way.

But there are other answers to Gregory's invitation, "Let us con-sider what kind of sacrifice this is for us." The message of liturgical renewal, I believe, is that there is something more to it — not that

---

[188] Gregory, *Dialogorum Libri Quatuor* 4.58, ed. A. Vogüé in *Sources chrétiennes* [=SC] 265 (1980) 200–2.

[189] Michael Heinlein, "An Early Image of a Mass of St Gregory and Devotion to the Holy Blood at Weingarten Abbey," *Gesta* 37 (1998) 55–62. Patricia DeLeeuw, "Unde et Memores, Domine: Memory and the Mass of St Gregory," *Memory and the Middle Ages*, ed. Nancy Netzer and Virginia Reinburg (Boston: Boston College Museum of Art 1995) 33–42. Pascal Mongne, "La messe de saint Grégoire du Musée des Jacobins d'Auch: une mosaïque de plumes mexicaines du XVIe siècle," *Revue du Louvre et des Musées de France* 43/5-6 [recte 44] (1994) 38–47. Flora Lewis, "Rewarding Devotion: Indulgences and the promotion of images," *The Church and the arts: papers read at the 1990 Summer Meeting and the 1991 Winter Meeting of the Ecclesiastical History Society*, ed. Diana Wood (Oxford: Blackwell 1992) 179–94. Uwe Westfehling, ed., *Die Messe Gregors des Grossen: Vision, Kunst, Realität: Katalog und Führer zu einer Ausstellung im Schnütgen-Museum der Stadt Köln* (Cologne: Das Museum 1982). Percy Dearmer, *Fifty Pictures of Gothic Altars*, Alcuin Club Collections 10 (London: Longmans, Green 1910) 86–87, 114–15, 162–63, 170–71, 206–7.

[190] Miri Rubin, *Corpus Christi: The Eucharist in Late Medieval Culture* (Cambridge: Cambridge University Press 1991) 63.

Human and Angelic Tongues

Gregory was wrong, but that something he didn't mention is also very important in principle, and today needs re-emphasizing in practice. That is, not only does the liturgy "save the soul from eternal destruction in a singular way" — it also brings us into a special relationship with each other, in the singular community that is the mystical body of Christ. People who value this aspect may prefer what might be called an "Augustinian" model of the Eucharist, for St Augustine (whose worship did not follow the Roman rite, by the way) eloquently described the spiritual union of sacrifice, redemption, and community that the faithful can recognize when the liturgy is regularly celebrated in a way that is accessible or familiar *[noto]* to them:

"True sacrifices are works of mercy (either toward ourselves or toward our neighbors) which are offered to God. . . . This happens especially when the whole redeemed city itself — that is the congregation and society of the saints — is offered to God as a universal sacrifice, by the great priest who, in the form of a servant, even offered himself for us during his passion, so that we might be the body of such a head. . . . This is the sacrifice of Christians: 'many are one body in Christ' (Romans 12:5). The Church continually reproduces this [sacrifice] in the sacrament of the altar — so familiar to the faithful — where it is shown forth to [the Church] that, in [the oblation] which [the Church] offers, [the Church] itself is offered."[191]

One way to read contemporary tensions about liturgical language, therefore, is to see in them the collision of a vaguely recalled "Gregorian" eucharistic model with a too-taken-for-granted "Augustinian" one. Like a fish who cannot grasp the concept of "water" because it cannot imagine swimming in anything else, the partisans of each side have trouble understanding the other's model, because they have not cultivated sufficient objective distance from their own. A way out would be to recognize that we are all faced with the classic Scholastic problem: two statements of unimpeachable authority that appear to disagree. It is not that Gregory contradicted Augustine, of course — in fact he read him with great respect. But for substantial and complex historical

---

[191] *De Civitate Dei* 10.6, ed. B. Dombart and A. Kalb, *CCL* 47 (1955) 278–79; also quoted in *Catechism of the Catholic Church* 1372.

reasons, each emphasized what seemed to be needed at the time, without denying the importance of other aspects that weren't mentioned. Neither father intended his description of the Eucharist to be exhaustive. What is needed in our time is the recognition that neither model should be taken in isolation as representing the "real" or complete tradition, but that the fullness of tradition is broader than either of them, and somehow balances both: diversity without adversity. Learning to look at the history of the Roman Mass through both optics at the same time, one begins to see the tradition more completely, coming to life in all four dimensions of space-time. From that perspective, our present fussing over liturgical language seems very myopic indeed.

Languages of the Sacred. Let's say, for the sake of argument, that C. S. Lewis was right — that it is not possible to have a liturgical language that is archaic, classical, Latinate, but also direct, colloquial, contemporary — at least not in the same celebration.[192] We would then have to choose one over the other. But to think we are actually limited to these two alternatives is, I say, to construe the liturgical tradition too narrowly. For example, if anyone will take a deep, calming breath and actually attend some celebrations that follow the pre-Vatican II Roman Missal (or at least buy a video from one of those "Tridentine Mass" groups), she or he will observe that quite a lot of its "message" is expressed without words at all. There is a language of kinesics or movement: gestures and positions of the hands and the eyes, graded degrees of bowing and genuflecting, turning to the people and turning east. There is a language of proxemics, or the use of space, as the ministers stand, kneel, and sit in a sequence of positions, expressing both their hierarchical relationships to each other and their reverence for the altar, the relics, the crucifix, the Gospels, the eucharistic vessels, and above all the consecrated bread and wine. And there is a paralanguage of non-verbal sound, with the trembling of bells at the approach of the *tremendum*, wooden clappers suggesting the

---

[192] I am, of course, ignoring such quiddities as the fact that we still recite the Our Father with the antiquated "who art in heaven" wording, but then end with the modern "For the kingdom, the power, and the glory are yours . . ." instead of the traditional "For thine is the kingdom."

dryness of the Lenten fast, three levels of speech volume, longer and shorter silences,[193] music that aims to be meditative more than emotive. In short the traditional Roman rite made ingenious use of the knowledge that "liturgy is not just information or teaching, whose only importance is its content. It is also symbolic action."[194]

The expressive potential of movement, gesture, closeness, and wordless sound is something we learn to use even before we learn verbal language, and thus it still speaks to us, at a profound level, of what is difficult to say in words.[195] As a developmental psychologist would put it, there are "different levels of understanding. . . . The first of these levels is *motoric* or *practical* understanding. This is the level of action. The child can act directly on objects and manipulate them correctly. . . . [He] has "understood" objects at the level of motor responses. . . . Another level of understanding is *conceptualization*. Here the child reconstructs internally the actions that were previously performed on objects, and at the same time adds new characteristics to these actions. He organizes the mental activities and provides logical connections. At the same time,

---

[193] On kinesics, proxemics and paralinguistics in general, see Mary Ritchie Key, *Nonverbal communication: A research guide and bibliography* (Metuchen, N.J.: Scarecrow Press 1977). Robert G. Harper et al., *Nonverbal Communication: The State of the Art* (New York: John Wiley 1978). Constance Obudho, *Human Nonverbal Behavior: An Annotated Bibliography* (Westport, CT: Greenwood Press 1979). Martha Davis and Janet Skupien, *Body Movement and Nonverbal Communication: An Annotated Bibliography, 1971–1981*, Advances in Semiotics (Bloomington: Indiana University Press 1982). Mary Ritchie Key, *Nonverbal Communication Today: Current Research*, Contributions to the Sociology of Language 33 (Amsterdam: Mouton Publishers 1982). Fernando Poyatos, ed., *Cross-Cultural Perspectives in Nonverbal Communication* (Lewiston, N.Y.: C. J. Hogrefe 1988). Robert S. Feldman and Bernard Rimé, eds., *Fundamentals of Nonverbal Behavior*, Studies in Emotion and Social Interaction (Cambridge: Cambridge University Press 1991). Joy Hendry and C. W. Watson, *An Anthropology of Indirect Communication*, Association of Social Anthropologists Monographs 37 (London: Routledge 2001).

[194] Gelineau, *The Liturgy Today and Tomorrow* 11, quoted in chapter 2 above, p. 53.

[195] David McNeill, *Hand and Mind: What Gestures Reveal about Thought* (Chicago: University of Chicago Press 1992). Lynn S. Messing and Ruth Campbell, eds., *Gesture, Speech, and Sign* (Oxford: Oxford University Press 1999). David McNeill, ed., *Language and Gesture* (Cambridge: Cambridge University Press 2000). Michael C. Corballis, "Did Language Evolve from Manual Gestures?" and Robbins Burling, "The Slow Growth of Language in Children," in *The Transition to Language*, ed. Alison Wray, Studies in the Evolution of Language (Oxford: Oxford University Press 2002) 161–79, 297–310.

Translating Tradition

much of the child's intellectual work remains unconscious. . . .
The child is often capable of mental operations that he is not aware
of and cannot express. A third level of knowledge involves *consciousness* and *verbalizations*. Now the child can deal with concepts
on an abstract level and can express his mental operations in words.
The child can reflect on his own thought."[196]

We should not think, however, that the more advanced types of
understanding supplant and eliminate the earlier kinds. A person
who has acquired language does not lose the capacity to understand at the more basic levels. People who have learned to read
still respond to imagery and narrative at the "conceptual" level,
dance and gesture at the "motoric" level. Indeed the ability to
contrast and combine these different kinds of understanding is a
major source of human creativity. Thus in recent decades, the
interdisciplinary and multicultural field of "performance studies"
has focused on the interaction of dance and movement with
imagery, narrative, mythology, and with the verbal arts of poetry,
song and drama.[197] There are even those who use performance to
teach written literature which is conventionally read individually
and silently.[198] As yet, however, there has been relatively little

---

[196] Herbert P. Ginsburg and Sylvia Opper, *Piaget's Theory of Intellectual Development*, 3rd ed. (Englewood Cliffs, N.J.: Prentice Hall 1988) 250 (italics original).

[197] For introductions and bibliography, see: Richard Bauman, ed., *Folklore,
Cultural Performances, and Popular Entertainment: A Communications-Centered Handbook* (New York: Oxford University Press 1992). Richard Schechner, "Ritual and
Performance," *Companion Encyclopedia of Anthropology*, ed. Tim Ingold (London:
Routledge 1994) 613–47. Henry Sayre, "Performance," *Critical Terms for Literary
Study*, 2nd ed., ed. Frank Lentricchia and Thomas McLaughlin (Chicago: University of Chicago Press 1995) 91–104. Catherine Bell, "Performance," *Critical Terms
for Religious Studies*, ed. Mark C. Taylor (Chicago: University of Chicago Press
1998) 205–24.

[198] "Performance forces us to evoke all of our experience with a text — our research into the meanings and significance of its words, our intellectual and emotional understanding of the speaker and the action in the text, and our physical
and vocal experience of the sounds. . . . In some way, we all 'perform' all the
time." Beverly Whitaker Long and Mary Frances Hopkins, *Performing Literature:
An Introduction to Oral Interpretation* (Englewood Cliffs, N.J.: Prentice Hall 1982)
xiii–xiv. For examples of historical study with attention to both performance
issues and textual transmission, see Arthur F. Marotti and Michael D. Bristol,
eds., *Print, Manuscript, Performance: The Changing Relations of the Media in Early
Modern England* (Columbus: Ohio State University Press 2000).

Human and Angelic Tongues

research into the performance history of the Roman liturgy, because (on the one hand) not many specialists in performance studies are sufficiently familiar with the theological and canonical primary sources,[199] and (on the other) ecclesiastical experts in liturgical law and theology are not trained to work in the "languages" of movement, space, and non-verbal media.

At the time of Vatican II, therefore, the dynamic of nonverbal communication was not well appreciated. People became liturgical experts by studying authoritative texts that had been established by methods of textual criticism. The proudest boast of the liturgical reformers was that their agenda was rooted in scholarly knowledge of these historical sources, privileging verbal understanding over any other kind, favoring practices that were mentioned in early texts over practices that were not, declaring that the correct meaning of any liturgical act was whatever research had determined to be its original function, with all subsequent understandings discredited. After the Council, the massive effort required to convert everything into vernacular only seemed to confirm the impression that liturgy is essentially text.

It is not surprising then, that most of what was not textual was expected to wither away. The liturgists of the time thought that all the bowing and genuflecting and "liturgical T-formations," the kissing of vessels and tracing of crosses in the air, had developed merely as a poor substitute for the textual intelligibility that was lost at whatever date Latin ceased to be understood by the laity (we still do not know when that was!). These things would scarcely be missed, they were sure, once intelligibility had been restored.[200]

---

[199] An interesting survey of medieval gesture, not sufficiently specialized in the area of liturgy, is Jean-Claude Schmitt, *La raison des gestes dans l'occident médiéval*, Bibliothèque des Histoires (Paris: Gallimard 1990), summarized in Schmitt, "The rationale of gestures in the West: third to thirteenth centuries," *A Cultural History of Gesture*, ed. Jan Bremmer and Herman Roodenburg (Ithaca, N.Y.: Cornell University Press 1992) 59–70. A number of medieval and modern treatises are reprinted in Jean Umiker-Sebeok and Thomas A. Sebeok, eds., *Monastic Sign Languages*, Approaches to Semiotics 76 (Berlin: Mouton de Gruyter 1987). I hope to write about the kinesic and proxemic aspects of the early Roman rite in a translation of and commentary on *Ordo Romanus I* that I am working on.

[200] A typical view from back then: "The only time when there arose in the West a strong appeal to 'mystery' as an important element in the Mass-liturgy was in

This impression seemed to be confirmed by the fact that many liturgical actions had acquired allegorical interpretations over the centuries that were provably at variance with their original functions. Not having studied the rituals of other world religions, the liturgical experts of those days did not know that bodily actions frequently appear more stable and resistant to change over time than the verbal explanations that emerge to account for them.[201] They thought the vernacular would render the meaning of the few remaining gestures self-evident, and that that would be enough.

What really happened, I submit, was that the reformers simply discarded what the only training available at the time had not taught them to appreciate. The ordinary clergy and people simply deferred to the experts, and the classically-trained musicians, who had an intuitive sense of liturgy-as-performance but were unable to articulate it in Vatican II terms, found themselves ostracized as part of the problem. The result is that even the non-verbal elements that remain in the new liturgy have been reshaped to fit verbal explanations of what they are supposed to mean or accomplish. A simple example: it was once the practice to genuflect on one knee when one knew the Blessed Sacrament to be present (in the

---

the Middle Ages. It was due, in part perhaps, to contact with the Eastern spirit and the struggle with Arianism; but it arose chiefly because of two things which took place in the West: the inability of the people to understand the Latin liturgy any longer, and the Eucharistic discussions which arose in the early Middle Ages, beginning especially with Isidore of Seville. These discussions laid special emphasis upon the divinity of Christ, and looked upon the Blessed Sacrament as a Supreme Gift of God, granted to us at the climactic moment of the Mass, the Consecration. The Middle Ages were entirely engrossed, in their theological discussions, with questions of this kind; the notion of the Mass as a sacrifice was not set forth with equal clarity." John L. Murphy, *The Mass and Liturgical Reform* (Milwaukee: Bruce Publishing Company 1956) 247.

[201] For example, one study argues that "elaborate models, coherent meanings, and consistent interpretations of the rite are things which people *may come to have*, through, and as a reaction to, performing it. These models do not underlie it." Caroline Humphrey and James Laidlaw, *The Archetypal Actions of Ritual: A Theory of Ritual Illustrated by the Jain Rite of Worship*, Oxford Studies in Social and Cultural Anthropology (Oxford: Clarendon Press 1994) 265, italics original. A range of recent studies on the verbal and non-verbal in ritual is discussed in Andrew Arno, "Aesthetics, Intuition, and Reference in Fijian Ritual Communication: Modularity in and out of Language," *American Anthropologist* 105 (2003) 807–19.

tabernacle, say), but to kneel on two knees when one could actually see the host, at the consecration during Mass or when exposed in a monstrance. However, since the 1973 document "Holy Communion and Worship of the Eucharist outside Mass" (84), one is to genuflect on one knee whether the Sacrament is reserved or exposed.[202] At the level of verbal understanding this is entirely sensible,[203] since the spiritual reality is the same: Christ is not "more present" in the exposed sacrament than in the reserved host. But the unintended consequence is that the experience of seeing no longer has any spiritual value, since one reacts the same way whether one sees or not. A hundred similar decisions, each reasonable in itself, have the cumulative effect of degrading all non-verbal behaviors that were once deeply experienced, creating a liturgy in which the people are fully participating only if they sing "Taste and see" — but not if they simply taste or see.

In my experience, one reason some people are attracted to the pre-Conciliar liturgy, or bored by the new one, is that they are particularly sensitive to what I once heard a preacher call "that Catholic wisdom that actions speak louder than words." It may seem absurd that liturgically sensitive people should feel alienated from a liturgy that tries so hard to reach out to people through everyday language and popular music. But that is because the renewal embodies the unstated assumption of many intellectuals that culture, including liturgy, is primarily verbal and linguistic — the same assumption that underlies much serious and scholarly writing on jazz, popular music, and folk song, which discusses only the words as if there isn't anything else. Yet a visit to any suburban mall will reveal how much time people choose to spend seeing and

---

[202] "unico genu flectitur," in *De sacra Communione et de Cultu Mysterii Eucharistici extra Missam* (Vatican City: Typis Polyglottis Vaticanis 1973) p. 38.

[203] If, that is, one ignores the inconsistency with the consecration itself, where the *General Instruction* does not say how many knees, and does not even require kneeling at all. The 1975 edition (21) says the people are to kneel "unless prevented by the lack of space, the number of people present, or some other good reason." The new edition (43) leaves the matter to episcopal conferences, but says that, where it is the custom for people to remain kneeling ("genuflexum manere") from the end of the Sanctus to the end of the Eucharistic Prayer, this is laudably retained.

Translating Tradition

tasting, and how much of popular culture — sports, fashion, dance, diet and health fads, cinema and TV — is visual and bodily.

Thus the old pre-Conciliar rite of Benediction, despite being mostly in Latin, may have been as close to popular culture as a 60s folk Mass with tunes from *Godspell*, though in a completely different way. By emphasizing what was visual, Benediction offered "the actual, immediate experience of seeing and responding" that one pioneering critic identified as central to modern film, a reality that too many intellectuals, "caught in the conflict between 'high culture' and 'popular culture,' have too often sought to evade." And it promised to fulfill the "very definite expectations" of the people who went to it, expectations that had been nurtured not by their daily "experience of reality" but by "previous experience of the [rite] itself: it creates its own field of reference."[204] Indeed the crass popular accretions that horrified the liturgically-informed of those days were unabashedly cinematic: brightening and dimming the lights to mark emotional crescendos and decrescendos, singing a lullaby to the Christ child as the host was lovingly put to bed in the tabernacle.[205]

My point, of course, is not that one type of worship is simply right and the other simply wrong. The either/or stance is the very thing I object to. Each kind of worship begins with an incomplete but not-illegitimate model of experiencing the divine presence: seeing the heavenly bread in one case, hearing the divine word in the other. But each, when overemphasized to the exclusion of alternatives, becomes increasingly distorted until it is ultimately a caricature. The same thing happens when ideological antagonists

---

[204] Robert Warshow, *The Immediate Experience: Movies, Comics, Theatre & Other Aspects of Popular Culture* (Garden City: Doubleday 1962; repr. New York: Atheneum 1979) 26, 130.

[205] H. A. Reinhold, *The American Parish and the Roman Liturgy: An Essay in Seven Chapters* (New York: Macmillan 1958) 11–12. In August 2003, searching "Good night, sweet Jesus" on the Web yielded several interesting memoirs, to which I cautiously refer the curious reader. Among them was one about "members of one American parish" who "were dismayed when their Bishop suppressed the old favorite which they had sung as the tabernacle was closed. . . . They appealed for exemption. This bishop granted it — provided that, as they sang it, the priest and people stood on their tiptoes and waved!" (www.hinet.net.au/~peterk/tiaabackground.html).

Human and Angelic Tongues

use a selective account of "tradition" as a weapon against their own co-religionists.

Obviously there were good reasons to reposition the liturgy upon the centrality of the life-giving word, so that it is now easier to see what was missing from Latin Benediction than it is to perceive clearly the drawbacks of what we are doing now. But like every other reform in history, our word-centered approach has provoked new and unforeseen difficulties that increasingly need addressing, and of which *LA* is a direct and regrettable result. One of these unintended problems is that, when the reformed liturgy is celebrated badly (as occasionally happens), it readily deteriorates into mere verbiage: one person after another reading texts out of books, relieved from time to time by unscripted chatter, followed by more reading from books. The esoteric fact that what is being read will be sometimes a sacramentary, other times a lectionary, or one of those monthly periodicals containing Prayers of the Faithful, the Bishop's Appeal or the parish announcements, makes no apparent difference at the bodily level of action or experience. The responsibility for keeping the celebration out of such doldrums sits squarely on the shoulders of the individual priest, though many priests (as liturgists ceaselessly complain) seem hardly up to the job. As a result, books have had to be written to tell priests how to act (as one would have it) "strong, loving, and wise."[206] Before the reform, on the other hand, this responsibility was borne by the rite itself. The rubrically mandated gestures and choreographed movements left no room for spontaneity, but they did ensure that the non-textual parts of the tradition remained minimally intact, even when (as occasionally happened) the priest in question was weak, spiteful, and borderline.

---

[206] Robert W. Hovda, *Strong, Loving and Wise: Presiding in Liturgy* (Washington, D.C.: The Liturgical Conference 1976). I do not wish to be perceived as attacking this book in particular, which may well be the best of its genre. My point is that the realization that "worship . . . is a body-thing, not a head-thing" (p. 92) is already expressed in the liturgical tradition itself. The notion that this dimension of worship is primarily to be handled by telling individual priests to work on their stage presence may be an improvement over "the faceless priest" approach recalled from "pre-Vatican II days" (p. v), but it does not begin to recover what was already present, unrecognized, in the full tradition.

Translating Tradition

Another unforeseen and unfortunate result of equating worship with word is that, when problems develop, textual remedies seem to be the only ones available. If some people think the church needs to be more gender-inclusive, the push for change has to focus on language. If other people think the liturgy isn't reverent enough, the only solution is to change the translation. With most of the non-verbals stripped out, there is nothing else left to fight over but the location of the tabernacle, the major surviving proxemic element. That is why the opening gun of *LA*'s "new era" is aimed directly at the texts. That is why those who disagree with *LA* feel they cannot afford to give in on language, or all will be lost.

To me, this kind of impasse is a sure sign that both sides are defining the tradition too narrowly, leaving no room for common ground. The way to broaden out again is for everyone to return to the sources and learn to recognize the fuller tradition, including the elements that are not particularly supportive of one's own preferences. With a renewed study of the complete history of the liturgy, in all its media, we could re-learn its languages of space and movement, sound and symbol, and make them "speak" of what needs saying today. Then we could have a liturgy that retains full intelligibility at the verbal level, but is also rich and moving and powerful — not to mention traditional — at the experiential and sensual and corporeal levels. And when new issues and dis-agreements emerged, there'd be a lot more room for compromise and conciliation.

Indeed the effort to develop such a multidimensional liturgy would have many benefits for the wider life of the church. For one thing, the field of liturgiology itself would have to expand. One can never know too many languages or texts, and the study of the historical sources should of course remain central. But liturgical scholars and leaders will also need to know how to work in an informed way with the parts that are not linguistic or textual. Important studies already exist, of course, that have enlisted anthropological or sociological theory in the study of liturgy. But the next generation of liturgists will need to know something about ethnographic techniques and qualitative research, and have significant exposure to fields like linguistics, psychology, sociology, archeology, and the history of the performing arts. When we consider the payoffs it doesn't seem like asking too much: Once liturgical specialists knew how to "read" a live celebration or a liturgical space, the critique of actual worship services could be based on participant observation and thick description, instead of mere anecdote or the mechanical application of regulations. Pastoral liturgists who knew how to use semi-structured interviewing, discourse analysis, and focus groups could tailor their ministry to the people and communities they are really working with, eliminating the kinds of confrontational dysfunction that have spawned rueful jokes about liturgists as terrorists.[207] Clerical stereotypes about lay people would no longer be dignified automatically with the label "pastoral," but would give way to field studies of how theologically-uneducated individuals actually do construct spiritual lives and "theology of the streets."[208]

Another benefit is that both research and teaching would have to deal seriously with the entire history of the liturgy. I own a shelf-full of books that promise to tell the whole story, but actually leapfrog from the patristic period to the liturgical movement, slighting a dozen or more centuries in between as a period of unrelieved superstition, decay, legalism, and general failure to grasp what liturgy is Really All About. But in fact the liturgy was a fount of Christian prayer and spirituality in every age, no matter how different it may have been from what we need or want today. All of us have much to learn from the full historical record, which is (after all) the heritage of every baptized person, not the private preserve of either scholars or ecclesiarchs. Indeed the Roman liturgy in particular is part of the cultural inheritance of the entire human race, and no one can foresee what creative re-uses the odd facts of the past may be put to in the near or distant future, as we

[207] Michael J. McCallion and David R. Maines, "Liturgical Problems and the Liturgist: On the Consequences of a New Occupation in the Catholic Church," *Unusual Occupations*, ed. Helena Z. Lopata and Kevin D. Henson, Current Research on Occupations and Professions 11 (Stamford, Connecticut: JAI Press 2000) 241–59, see p. 242. Compare Paul C. Rosenblatt, "Qualitative research as a spiritual experience," *The Emotional Nature of Qualitative Research*, ed. Kathleen R. Gilbert, Innovations in Psychology (Boca Raton, Florida: CRC Press 2001) 111–28.

[208] Robert Anthony Orsi, *The Madonna of 115th Street: Faith and Community in Italian Harlem, 1880–1950* (New Haven: Yale University Press 1985) 219. See also Orlando O. Espín, *The Faith of the People: Theological Reflections on Popular Catholicism* (Maryknoll, N.Y.: Orbis Books 1997).

recover the etymological meaning of liturgy as "the work of the people."

Finally, of course, a large repertory of resources would become available for dealing with the kinds of problems *LA* identifies and exemplifies, showing that one of the best ways to deal with controversy in the present is by broadened understanding and honest acknowledgement of the past. A wider and deeper knowledge of liturgical history would reveal that many of our problems and disagreements are not new, and that an extensive array of solutions has been tried over many centuries, offering significant and informative precedents for many of today's proposals. Partisan narrowing of the received tradition would be recognized more readily as the unjust tactic it actually is. Firebrands would have to be more humble about the self-evident rightness of their own positions, while people of good will would have more room in which to seek workable compromises.

The emphasis, then, should be on the wholeness that is at the heart of Catholicism. A tradition that puts as high a value as we do on the integrity of the whole human person needs a worship that operates at every level of human understanding, teaching people to love God with the whole heart and the whole soul and the whole mind (Mark 12:30), enjoying the riches of all human societies and cultures. The lack of such integration right now is the cause of much of our suffering. For a wholesome vision of the Catholic tradition, of diversity affirming unity, we can return once more to the letter of Anselm of Laon, quoted above. Within it there is an implicit exegesis that speaks to the very nature of Catholicism, based on St Paul's question, "So if the whole church meets in one place and everyone speaks in tongues, and then uninstructed people or unbelievers should come in, will they not say that you are out of your minds?" (1 Corinthians 14:23). That is, indeed, what much of the world does say about us, and no wonder. In the Latin Vulgate, which Anselm quoted only partially, this begins *Si ergo conveniat universa ecclesia in unum:* "If, therefore, the universal church comes together as one." In the literal sense, no doubt, Paul was thinking only of the local Corinthian congregation; the original Greek says *hē ekklēsia holē:* "the whole church." But the Greek word *holos, holē* is also the root of the word "Catholic." Already in the New Testament we can observe a sense that the local congregations could be spoken of as forming a larger entity, "the Church" in the singular, not the plural, as in "The Church throughout all Judea, Galilee, and Samaria was at peace" (Acts 9:31). It didn't take long for the prepositional phrase "throughout all" or "throughout the whole" *(hē ekklēsia kath' holēs)* to become the adjective "catholic," modifying "church" *(hē ekklēsia katholikē)*, so that in the second century "the Church of God dwelling in Smyrna" could send its account of St Polycarp's martyrdom "to all the dwellings of the holy and throughout-the-whole church in every place," and St Ignatius of Antioch could write to the Smyrneans, "Where Christ is, there is the throughout-the-whole church."[209]

Thus the Catholic Church is something more than a federation of local churches, yet also something more than a worldwide diocese of Rome. It is a mystery of an incarnational kind, so that somehow the whole body is present whenever the local church assembles, the whole Christ prays when the local church worships. That is why Anselm could find a deeper meaning in St Paul's reference to the Corinthian assemblies: "The statements of all the Catholic Fathers are diverse but not adverse, they concur by 'coming together as one'." For us too, the Catholic tradition, fully acknowledged and properly understood, should be our place of coming together, not of coming apart. It is a great tradition that has contributed generously to the artistic and spiritual treasury of all humanity, a many-sided dialogue in which issues of heritage, creativity, and cultural adaptation have always been central. It offers models and examples for reconciling diversity into unity without adversity. And it has two thousand years experience — not forty — wrestling with issues of language, translation, and cultural expression.

---

[209] *Martyrium Polycarpi*, titulus. Ignatius, *Ad Smyrnaeos* 8. *Die apostolischen Väter* 1, ed. Karl Bihlmeyer and Wilhelm Schneemelcher, 3rd ed. (Tübingen: J.C.B. Mohr 1970) 120, 108.

Appendix

English translation of *Liturgiam Authenticam*

CONGREGATION FOR DIVINE WORSHIP
AND THE DISCIPLINE OF THE SACRAMENTS

FIFTH INSTRUCTION
"FOR THE RIGHT IMPLEMENTATION
OF THE CONSTITUTION ON THE SACRED LITURGY
OF THE SECOND VATICAN COUNCIL"
(*Sacrosanctum Concilium*, art. 36)

Liturgiam authenticam
ON THE USE OF VERNACULAR LANGUAGES
IN THE PUBLICATION OF
THE BOOKS OF THE ROMAN LITURGY

1. The Second Vatican Council strongly desired to preserve with care the authentic Liturgy, which flows forth from the Church's living and most ancient spiritual tradition, and to adapt it with pastoral wisdom to the genius of the various peoples so that the faithful might find in their full, conscious, and active participation in the sacred actions — especially the celebration of the Sacraments — an abundant source of graces and a means for their own continual formation in the Christian mystery.[1]

2. Thereupon there began, under the care of the Supreme Pontiffs, the great work of renewal of the liturgical books of the Roman Rite, a work which included their translation[2] into vernacular languages, with the purpose of bringing about in the most diligent way that renewal of the sacred Liturgy which was one of the foremost intentions of the Council.

3. The liturgical renewal thus far has seen positive results, achieved through the labor and the skill of many, but in particular of the Bishops, to whose care and zeal this great and difficult charge is entrusted. Even so, the greatest prudence and attention is required in the preparation of liturgical books marked by sound doctrine, which are exact in wording, free from all ideological influence, and otherwise endowed with those qualities by which the sacred mysteries of salvation and the indefectible faith of the Church are efficaciously transmitted by means of human language to prayer, and worthy worship is offered to God the Most High.[3]

Appendix

4. The Second Vatican Ecumenical Council in its deliberations and decrees assigned a singular importance to the liturgical rites, the ecclesiastical traditions, and the discipline of Christian life proper to those particular Churches, especially of the East, which are distinguished by their venerable antiquity, manifesting in various ways the tradition received through the Fathers from the Apostles.[4] The Council asked that the traditions of each of these particular Churches be preserved whole and intact. For this reason, even while calling for the revision of the various Rites in accordance with sound tradition, the Council set forth the principle that only those changes were to be introduced which would foster their specific organic development.[5] Clearly, the same vigilance is required for the safeguarding and the authentic development of the liturgical rites, the ecclesiastical traditions, and the discipline of the Latin Church, and in particular, of the Roman Rite. The same care must be brought also to the translation of the liturgical texts into vernacular languages. This is especially true as regards the Roman Missal, which will thus continue to be maintained as an outstanding sign and instrument of the integrity and unity of the Roman Rite.[6]

5. Indeed, it may be affirmed that the Roman Rite is itself a precious example and an instrument of true inculturation. For the Roman Rite is marked by a signal capacity for assimilating into itself spoken and sung texts, gestures and rites derived from the customs and the genius of diverse nations and particular Churches — both Eastern and Western — into a harmonious unity that transcends the boundaries of any single region.[7] This characteristic is particularly evident in its orations, which exhibit a capacity to transcend the limits of their original situation so as to become the prayers of Christians in any time or place. In preparing all translations of the liturgical books, the greatest care is to be taken to maintain the identity and unitary expression of the Roman Rite,[8] not as a sort of historical monument, but rather as a manifestation of the theological realities of ecclesial communion and unity.[9] The work of inculturation, of which the translation into vernacular languages is a part, is not therefore to be considered an avenue for the creation of new varieties or families of rites; on the contrary, it should be recognized that any adaptations introduced out of cultural or pastoral necessity thereby become part of the Roman Rite, and are to be inserted into it in a harmonious way.[10]

6. Ever since the promulgation of the Constitution on the Sacred Liturgy, the work of the translation of the liturgical texts into vernacular languages, as promoted by the Apostolic See, has involved the publication of norms and the communication to the Bishops of advice on the matter. Nevertheless, it has been noted that translations of liturgical texts in various locali-

ties stand in need of improvement through correction or through a new draft.[11] The omissions or errors which affect certain existing vernacular translations — especially in the case of certain languages — have impeded the progress of the inculturation that actually should have taken place. Consequently, the Church has been prevented from laying the foundation for a fuller, healthier and more authentic renewal.

7. For these reasons, it now seems necessary to set forth anew, and in light of the maturing of experience, the principles of translation to be followed in future translations — whether they be entirely new undertakings or emendations of texts already in use — and to specify more clearly certain norms that have already been published, taking into account a number of questions and circumstances that have arisen in our own day. In order to take full advantage of the experience gained since the Council, it seems useful to express these norms from time to time in terms of tendencies that have been evident in past translations, but which are to be avoided in future ones. In fact, it seems necessary to consider anew the true notion of liturgical translation in order that the translations of the Sacred Liturgy into the vernacular languages may stand secure as the authentic voice of the Church of God.[12] This Instruction therefore envisions and seeks to prepare for a new era of liturgical renewal, which is consonant with the qualities and the traditions of the particular Churches, but which safeguards also the faith and the unity of the whole Church of God.

8. The norms set forth in this Instruction are to be substituted for all norms previously published on the matter, with the exception of the Instruction *Varietates legitimae*, published by the Congregation for Divine Worship and the Discipline of the Sacraments on 25 January 1994, in conjunction with which the norms in this present Instruction are to be understood.[13] The norms contained in this Instruction are to be considered applicable to the translation of texts intended for liturgical use in the Roman Rite and, *mutatis mutandis*, in the other duly recognized Rites of the Latin Church.

9. When it may be deemed appropriate by the Congregation for Divine Worship and the Discipline of the Sacraments, a text will be prepared after consultation with Bishops, called a *"ratio translationis,"* to be set forth by the authority of the same Dicastery, in which the principles of translation found in this Instruction will be applied in closer detail to a given language. This document may be composed of various elements as the situation may require, such as, for example, a list of vernacular words to be equated with their Latin counterparts, the setting forth of principles applicable specifically to a given language, and so forth.

Appendix

I
ON THE CHOICE OF VERNACULAR LANGUAGES
TO BE INTRODUCED INTO LITURGICAL USE

10. To be considered first of all is the choice of the languages that it will be permissible to put into use in liturgical celebrations. It is appropriate that there be elaborated in each territory a pastoral plan that takes account of the spoken languages there in use, with a distinction being made between languages which the people spontaneously speak and those which, not being used for natural communication in pastoral activity, merely remain the object of cultural interest. In considering and drafting such a plan, due caution should be exercised lest the faithful be fragmented into small groups by means of the selection of vernacular languages to be introduced into liturgical use, with the consequent danger of fomenting civil discord, to the detriment of the unity of peoples as well as of the unity of the particular Churches and the Church universal.

11. In this plan, a clear distinction is to be made also between those languages, on the one hand, that are used universally in the territory for pastoral communication, and those, on the other hand, that are to be used in the Sacred Liturgy. In drawing up the plan, it will be necessary to take account also of the question of the resources necessary for supporting the use of a given language, such as the number of priests, deacons and lay collaborators capable of using the language, in addition to the number of experts and those trained for and capable of preparing translations of all of the liturgical books of the Roman Rite in accord with the principles enunciated here. Also to be considered are the financial and technical resources necessary for preparing translations and printing books truly worthy of liturgical use.

12. Within the liturgical sphere, moreover, a distinction necessarily arises between languages and dialects. In particular, dialects that do not support common academic and cultural formation cannot be taken into full liturgical use, since they lack that stability and breadth that would be required for their being liturgical languages on a broader scale. In any event, the number of individual liturgical languages is not to be increased too greatly.[14] This latter is necessary so that a certain unity of language may be fostered within the boundaries of one and the same nation.

13. Moreover, the fact that a language is not introduced into full liturgical use does not mean that it is thereby altogether excluded from the Liturgy. It may be used, at least occasionally, in the Prayer of the Faithful, in the sung texts, in the invitations or instructions given to the people, or in parts

of the homily, especially if the language is proper to some of Christ's faithful who are in attendance. Nevertheless, it is always possible to use either the Latin language or another language that is widely used in that country, even if perhaps it may not be the language of all — or even of a majority — of the Christian faithful taking part, provided that discord among the faithful be avoided.

14. Since the introduction of languages into liturgical use by the Church may actually affect the development of the language itself and may even be determinative in its regard, care is to be taken to promote those languages which — even while perhaps lacking a long literary tradition — seem capable of being employed by a greater number of persons. It is necessary to avoid any fragmentation of dialects, especially at the moment when a given dialect may be passing from spoken to written form. Instead, care should be taken to foster and to develop forms of speech that are common to human communities.

15. It will be the responsibility of the Conference of Bishops to determine which of the prevailing languages are to be introduced into full or partial liturgical use in its territory. Their decisions require the *recognitio* of the Apostolic See before the work of translation is undertaken in any way.[15] Before giving its decision on this matter, the Conference of Bishops should not omit to seek the written opinion of experts and other collaborators in the work; these opinions, together with the other acts, are to be sent in written form to the Congregation for Divine Worship and the Discipline of the Sacraments, in addition to the *relatio* mentioned below, in art. n. 16.

16. As regards the decision of the Conference of Bishops for the introduction of a vernacular language into liturgical use, the following are to be observed (cf. n. 79):[16]

a) For the legitimate passage of decrees, a two-thirds vote by secret ballot is required on the part of those in the Conference of Bishops who have the right to cast a deliberative vote;

b) All of the acts to be examined by the Apostolic See, prepared in duplicate, signed by the President and Secretary of the Conference and duly affixed with its seal, are to be sent to the Congregation for Divine Worship and the Discipline of the Sacraments. In these acts are to be contained the following:

    i) the names of the Bishops, or of those equivalent to them in law, who were present at the meeting,

ii) a report of the proceedings, which should contain the outcome of the votes pertaining to the individual decrees, including the number of those in favor, the number opposed, and the number abstaining;

iii) a clear exposition of the individual parts of the Liturgy into which the decision has been made to introduce the vernacular language;

c) In the *relatio* is to be included a clear explanation of the language involved, as well as the reasons for which the proposal has been made to introduce it into liturgical use.

17. As for the use of "artificial" languages, proposed from time to time, the approval of texts as well as the granting of permission for their use in liturgical celebrations is strictly reserved to the Holy See. This faculty will be granted only for particular circumstances and for the pastoral good of the faithful, after consultation with the Bishops principally involved.[17]

18. In celebrations for speakers of a foreign language, such as visitors, migrants, pilgrims, etc., it is permissible, with the consent of the diocesan Bishop, to celebrate the Sacred Liturgy in a vernacular language known to these people, using a liturgical book already approved by the competent authority with the subsequent *recognitio* of the Apostolic See.[18] If such celebrations recur with some frequency, the diocesan Bishop is to send a brief report to the Congregation for Divine Worship and the Discipline of the Sacraments, describing the circumstances, the number of participants, and the editions used.

II
ON THE TRANSLATION OF LITURGICAL TEXTS INTO VERNACULAR LANGUAGES

1. General principles applicable to all translation

19. The words of the Sacred Scriptures, as well as the other words spoken in liturgical celebrations, especially in the celebration of the Sacraments, are not intended primarily to be a sort of mirror of the interior dispositions of the faithful; rather, they express truths that transcend the limits of time and space. Indeed, by means of these words God speaks continually with the Spouse of his beloved Son, the Holy Spirit leads the Christian faithful into all truth and causes the word of Christ to dwell abundantly within them, and the Church perpetuates and transmits all that she

herself is and all that she believes, even as she offers the prayers of all the faithful to God, through Christ and in the power of the Holy Spirit.[19]

20. The Latin liturgical texts of the Roman Rite, while drawing on centuries of ecclesial experience in transmitting the faith of the Church received from the Fathers, are themselves the fruit of the liturgical renewal, just recently brought forth. In order that such a rich patrimony may be preserved and passed on through the centuries, it is to be kept in mind from the beginning that the translation of the liturgical texts of the Roman Liturgy is not so much a work of creative innovation as it is of rendering the original texts faithfully and accurately into the vernacular language. While it is permissible to arrange the wording, the syntax and the style in such a way as to prepare a flowing vernacular text suitable to the rhythm of popular prayer, the original text, insofar as possible, must be translated integrally and in the most exact manner, without omissions or additions in terms of their content, and without paraphrases or glosses. Any adaptation to the characteristics or the nature of the various vernacular languages is to be sober and discreet.[20]

21. Especially in the translations intended for peoples recently brought to the Christian Faith, fidelity and exactness with respect to the original texts may themselves sometimes require that words already in current usage be employed in new ways, that new words or expressions be coined, that terms in the original text be transliterated or adapted to the pronunciation of the vernacular language,[21] or that figures of speech be used which convey in an integral manner the content of the Latin expression even while being verbally or syntactically different from it. Such measures, especially those of greater moment, are to be submitted to the discussion of all the Bishops involved before being inserted into the definitive draft. In particular, caution should be exercised in introducing words drawn from non-Christian religions.[22]

22. Adaptations of the texts according to articles 37-40 of the Constitution *Sacrosanctum Concilium* are to be considered on the basis of true cultural or pastoral necessity, and should not be proposed out of a mere desire for novelty or variety, nor as a way of supplementing or changing the theological content of the *editiones typicae*; rather, they are to be governed by the norms and procedures contained in the above-mentioned Instruction *Varietates legitimae*.[23] Accordingly, translations into vernacular languages that are sent to the Congregation for Divine Worship and the Discipline of the Sacraments for the *recognitio* are to contain, in addition to the translation itself and any adaptations foreseen explicitly in the *editiones typicae*,

only adaptations or modifications for which prior written consent has been obtained from the same Dicastery.

23. In the translation of texts of ecclesiastical composition, while it is useful with the assistance of historical and other scientific tools to consult a source that may have been discovered for the same text, nevertheless it is always the text of the Latin *editio typica* itself that is to be translated.

Whenever the biblical or liturgical text preserves words taken from other ancient languages (as, for example, the words *Alleluia* and *Amen*, the Aramaic words contained in the New Testament, the Greek words drawn from the *Trisagion* which are recited in the *Improperia* of Good Friday, and the *Kyrie eleison* of the Order of Mass, as well as many proper names) consideration should be given to preserving the same words in the new vernacular translation, at least as one option among others. Indeed, a careful respect for the original text will sometimes require that this be done.

24. Furthermore, it is not permissible that the translations be produced from other translations already made into other languages; rather, the new translations must be made directly from the original texts, namely the Latin, as regards the texts of ecclesiastical composition, or the Hebrew, Aramaic, or Greek, as the case may be, as regards the texts of Sacred Scripture.[24] Furthermore, in the preparation of these translations for liturgical use, the *Nova Vulgata Editio,* promulgated by the Apostolic See, is normally to be consulted as an auxiliary tool, in a manner described elsewhere in this Instruction, in order to maintain the tradition of interpretation that is proper to the Latin Liturgy.

25. So that the content of the original texts may be evident and comprehensible even to the faithful who lack any special intellectual formation, the translations should be characterized by a kind of language which is easily understandable, yet which at the same time preserves these texts' dignity, beauty, and doctrinal precision.[25] By means of words of praise and adoration that foster reverence and gratitude in the face of God's majesty, his power, his mercy and his transcendent nature, the translations will respond to the hunger and thirst for the living God that is experienced by the people of our own time, while contributing also to the dignity and beauty of the liturgical celebration itself.[26]

26. The liturgical texts' character as a very powerful instrument for instilling in the lives of the Christian faithful the elements of faith and Christian morality,[27] is to be maintained in the translations with the utmost

solicitude. The translation, furthermore, must always be in accord with sound doctrine.

27. Even if expressions should be avoided which hinder comprehension because of their excessively unusual or awkward nature, the liturgical texts should be considered as the voice of the Church at prayer, rather than of only particular congregations or individuals; thus, they should be free of an overly servile adherence to prevailing modes of expression. If indeed, in the liturgical texts, words or expressions are sometimes employed which differ somewhat from usual and everyday speech, it is often enough by virtue of this very fact that the texts become truly memorable and capable of expressing heavenly realities. Indeed, it will be seen that the observance of the principles set forth in this Instruction will contribute to the gradual development, in each vernacular, of a sacred style that will come to be recognized as proper to liturgical language. Thus it may happen that a certain manner of speech which has come to be considered somewhat obsolete in daily usage may continue to be maintained in the liturgical context. In translating biblical passages where seemingly inelegant words or expressions are used, a hasty tendency to sanitize this characteristic is likewise to be avoided. These principles, in fact, should free the Liturgy from the necessity of frequent revisions when modes of expression may have passed out of popular usage.

28. The Sacred Liturgy engages not only man's intellect, but the whole person, who is the "subject" of full and conscious participation in the liturgical celebration. Translators should therefore allow the signs and images of the texts, as well as the ritual actions, to speak for themselves; they should not attempt to render too explicit that which is implicit in the original texts. For the same reason, the addition of explanatory texts not contained in the *editio typica* is to be prudently avoided. Consideration should also be given to including in the vernacular editions at least some texts in the Latin language, especially those from the priceless treasury of Gregorian chant, which the Church recognizes as proper to the Roman Liturgy, and which, all other things being equal, is to be given pride of place in liturgical celebrations.[28] Such chant, indeed, has a great power to lift the human spirit to heavenly realities.

29. It is the task of the homily and of catechesis to set forth the meaning of the liturgical texts,[29] illuminating with precision the Church's understanding regarding the members of particular Churches or ecclesial communities separated from full communion with the Catholic Church and those of Jewish communities, as well as adherents of other religions — and likewise, her understanding of the dignity and equality of all men.[30] Similarly,

it is the task of catechists or of the homilist to transmit that right interpretation of the texts that excludes any prejudice or unjust discrimination on the basis of persons, gender, social condition, race or other criteria, which has no foundation at all in the texts of the Sacred Liturgy. Although considerations such as these may sometimes help one in choosing among various translations of a certain expression, they are not to be considered reasons for altering either a biblical text or a liturgical text that has been duly promulgated.

30. In many languages there exist nouns and pronouns denoting both genders, masculine and feminine, together in a single term. The insistence that such a usage should be changed is not necessarily to be regarded as the effect or the manifestation of an authentic development of the language as such. Even if it may be necessary by means of catechesis to ensure that such words continue to be understood in the "inclusive" sense just described, it may not be possible to employ different words in the translations themselves without detriment to the precise intended meaning of the text, the correlation of its various words or expressions, or its aesthetic qualities. When the original text, for example, employs a single term in expressing the interplay between the individual and the universality and unity of the human family or community (such as the Hebrew word 'adam, the Greek anthropos, or the Latin homo), this property of the language of the original text should be maintained in the translation. Just as has occurred at other times in history, the Church herself must freely decide upon the system of language that will serve her doctrinal mission most effectively, and should not be subject to externally imposed linguistic norms that are detrimental to that mission.

31. In particular: to be avoided is the systematic resort to imprudent solutions such as a mechanical substitution of words, the transition from the singular to the plural, the splitting of a unitary collective term into masculine and feminine parts, or the introduction of impersonal or abstract words, all of which may impede the communication of the true and integral sense of a word or an expression in the original text. Such measures introduce theological and anthropological problems into the translation. Some particular norms are the following:

a) In referring to almighty God or the individual persons of the Most Holy Trinity, the truth of tradition as well as the established gender usage of each respective language are to be maintained.

b) Particular care is to be taken to ensure that the fixed expression "Son of Man" be rendered faithfully and exactly. The great Christological and typological significance of this expression requires that there should also be employed throughout the translation a rule of language that will ensure that the fixed expression remain comprehensible in the context of the whole translation.

c) The term "fathers," found in many biblical passages and liturgical texts of ecclesiastical composition, is to be rendered by the corresponding masculine word into vernacular languages insofar as it may be seen to refer to the Patriarchs or the kings of the chosen people in the Old Testament, or to the Fathers of the Church.

d) Insofar as possible in a given vernacular language, the use of the feminine pronoun, rather than the neuter, is to be maintained in referring to the Church.

e) Words which express consanguinity or other important types of relationship, such as "brother," "sister," etc., which are clearly masculine or feminine by virtue of the context, are to be maintained as such in the translation.

f) The grammatical gender of angels, demons, and pagan gods or goddesses, according to the original texts, is to be maintained in the vernacular language insofar as possible.

g) In all these matters it will be necessary to remain attentive to the principles set forth above, in nn. 27 and 29.

32. The translation should not restrict the full sense of the original text within narrower limits. To be avoided on this account are expressions characteristic of commercial publicity, political or ideological programs, passing fashions, and those which are subject to regional variations or ambiguities in meaning. Academic style manuals or similar works, since they sometimes give way to such tendencies, are not to be considered standards for liturgical translation. On the other hand, works that are commonly considered "classics" in a given vernacular language may prove useful in providing a suitable standard for its vocabulary and usage.

33. The use of capitalization in the liturgical texts of the Latin *editiones typicae* as well as in the liturgical translation of the Sacred Scriptures, for honorific or otherwise theologically significant reasons, is to be retained in the vernacular language at least insofar as the structure of a given language permits.

34. It is preferable that a version of the Sacred Scriptures be prepared in accordance with the principles of sound exegesis and of high literary quality, but also with a view to the particular exigencies of liturgical use as regards style, the selection of words, and the selection from among different possible interpretations.

35. Wherever no such version of the Sacred Scriptures exists in a given language, it will be necessary to use a previously prepared version, while modifying the translation wherever appropriate so that it may be suitable for use in the liturgical context according to the principles set forth in this Instruction.

36. In order that the faithful may be able to commit to memory at least the more important texts of the Sacred Scriptures and be formed by them even in their private prayer, it is of the greatest importance that the translation of the Sacred Scriptures intended for liturgical use be characterized by a certain uniformity and stability, such that in every territory there should exist only one approved translation, which will be employed in all parts of the various liturgical books. This stability is especially to be desired in the translation of the Sacred Books of more frequent use, such as the Psalter, which is the fundamental prayer book of the Christian people.[31] The Conferences of Bishops are strongly encouraged to provide for the commissioning and publication in their territories of an integral translation of the Sacred Scriptures intended for the private study and reading of the faithful, which corresponds in every part to the text that is used in the Sacred Liturgy.

37. If the biblical translation from which the Lectionary is composed exhibits readings that differ from those set forth in the Latin liturgical text, it should be borne in mind that the *Nova Vulgata Editio* is the point of reference as regards the delineation of the canonical text.[32] Thus, in the translation of the deuterocanonical books and wherever else there may exist varying manuscript traditions, the liturgical translation must be prepared in accordance with the same manuscript tradition that the *Nova Vulgata* has followed. If a previously prepared translation reflects a choice that departs from that which is found in the *Nova Vulgata Editio* as regards the underlying textual tradition, the order of verses, or similar factors, the discrepancy needs to be remedied in the preparation of any Lectionary so that conformity with the Latin liturgical text may be maintained. In preparing new translations, it would be helpful, though not

Translating Tradition

obligatory, that the numbering of the verses also follow that of the same text as closely as possible.

38. It is often permissible that a variant reading of a verse be used, on the basis of critical editions and upon the recommendation of experts. However, this is not permissible in the case of a liturgical text where such a choice would affect those elements of the passage that are pertinent to its liturgical context, or whenever the principles found elsewhere in this Instruction would otherwise be neglected. For passages where a critical consensus is lacking, particular attention should be given to the choices reflected in the approved Latin text.[33]

39. The delineation of the biblical *pericopai* is to conform entirely to the *Ordo lectionum Missae* or to the other approved and confirmed liturgical texts, as the case may be.

40. With due regard for the requirements of sound exegesis, all care is to be taken to ensure that the words of the biblical passages commonly used in catechesis and in popular devotional prayers be maintained. On the other hand, great caution is to be taken to avoid a wording or style that the Catholic faithful would confuse with the manner of speech of non-Catholic ecclesial communities or of other religions, so that such a factor will not cause them confusion or discomfort.

41. The effort should be made to ensure that the translations be conformed to that understanding of biblical passages which has been handed down by liturgical use and by the tradition of the Fathers of the Church, especially as regards very important texts such as the Psalms and the readings used for the principal celebrations of the liturgical year; in these cases the greatest care is to be taken so that the translation express the traditional Christological, typological and spiritual sense, and manifest the unity and the inter-relatedness of the two Testaments.[34] For this reason:

a) it is advantageous to be guided by the *Nova Vulgata* wherever there is a need to choose, from among various possibilities [of translation], that one which is most suited for expressing the manner in which a text has traditionally been read and received within the Latin liturgical tradition;

b) for the same purpose, other ancient versions of the Sacred Scriptures should also be consulted, such as the Greek version of the Old Testament commonly known as the "Septuagint," which has been used by the Christian faithful from the earliest days of the Church;[35]

c) in accordance with immemorial tradition, which indeed is already evident in the above-mentioned "Septuagint" version, the name of almighty God expressed by the Hebrew *tetragrammaton* (YHWH) and rendered in Latin by the word *Dominus*, is to be rendered into any given vernacular by a word equivalent in meaning.

Finally, translators are strongly encouraged to pay close attention to the history of interpretation that may be drawn from citations of biblical texts in the writings of the Fathers of the Church, and also from those biblical images more frequently found in Christian art and hymnody.

42. While caution is advisable lest the historical context of the biblical passages be obscured, the translator should also bear in mind that the word of God proclaimed in the Liturgy is not simply an historical document. For the biblical text treats not only of the great persons and events of the Old and New Testaments, but also of the mysteries of salvation, and thus refers to the faithful of the present age and to their lives. While always maintaining due regard for the norm of fidelity to the original text, one should strive, whenever there is a choice to be made between different ways of translating a term, to make those choices that will enable the hearer to recognize himself and the dimensions of his own life as vividly as possible in the persons and events found in the text.

43. Modes of speech by which heavenly realities and actions are depicted in human form, or designated by means of limited, concrete terminology — as happens quite frequently in biblical language (i.e., anthropomorphisms) — often maintain their full force only if translated somewhat literally, as in the case of words in the *Nova Vulgata Editio* such as *ambulare, brachium, digitus, manus,* or *vultus [Dei],* as well as *caro, cornu, os, semen,* and *visitare.* Thus it is best that such terms not be explained or interpreted by more abstract or general vernacular expressions. As regards certain terms, such as those translated in the *Nova Vulgata* as *anima* and *spiritus,* the principles mentioned in above nn. 40-41 should be observed. Therefore, one should avoid replacing these terms by a personal pronoun or a more abstract term, except when this is strictly necessary in a given case. It should be borne in mind that a literal translation of terms which may initially sound odd in a vernacular language may for this very reason provoke inquisitiveness in the hearer and provide an occasion for catechesis.

44. In order for a translation to be more easily proclaimed, it is necessary that any expression be avoided which is confusing or ambiguous when heard, such that the hearer would fail to grasp its meaning.

Translating Tradition

45. Apart from that which is set forth in the *Ordo lectionum Missae,* the following norms are to be observed in the preparation of a Lectionary of biblical readings in a vernacular language:

a) Passages of Sacred Scripture contained in the *Praenotanda* of the *Ordo lectionum Missae* are to conform completely to the translation of the same passages as they occur within the Lectionary.

b) Likewise the titles, expressing the theme of the readings and placed at the head of them, are to retain the wording of the readings themselves, wherever such a correspondence exists in the *Ordo lectionum Missae.*

c) Finally, the words prescribed by the *Ordo lectionum Missae* for the beginning of the reading, called the *incipits,* are to follow as closely as possible the wording of the vernacular biblical version from which the readings are generally taken, refraining from following other translations. As regards those parts of the *incipits* that are not part of the biblical text itself, these are to be translated exactly from the Latin when preparing Lectionaries, unless the Conference of Bishops shall have sought and obtained the prior consent of the Congregation for Divine Worship and the Discipline of the Sacraments authorizing a different procedure for introducing the readings.

3. NORMS CONCERNING THE TRANSLATION OF OTHER LITURGICAL TEXTS

46. The norms set forth above, and those regarding Sacred Scripture, should be applied, *mutatis mutandis,* in like manner to the texts of ecclesiastical composition.

47. While the translation must transmit the perennial treasury of orations by means of language understandable in the cultural context for which it is intended, it should also be guided by the conviction that liturgical prayer not only is formed by the genius of a culture, but itself contributes to the development of that culture. Consequently it should cause no surprise that such language differs somewhat from ordinary speech. Liturgical translation that takes due account of the authority and integral content of the original texts will facilitate the development of a sacral vernacular, characterized by a vocabulary, syntax and grammar that are proper to divine worship, even though it is not to be excluded that it may exercise an influence even on everyday speech, as has occurred in the languages of peoples evangelized long ago.

48. The texts for the principal celebrations occurring throughout the liturgical year should be offered to the faithful in a translation that is

easily committed to memory, so as to render them usable in private prayers as well.

A. Vocabulary

49. Characteristic of the orations of the Roman liturgical tradition as well as of the other Catholic Rites is a coherent system of words and patterns of speech, consecrated by the books of Sacred Scripture and by ecclesial tradition, especially the writings of the Fathers of the Church. For this reason the manner of translating the liturgical books should foster a correspondence between the biblical text itself and the liturgical texts of ecclesiastical composition which contain biblical words or allusions.[36] In the translation of such texts, the translator would best be guided by the manner of expression that is characteristic of the version of the Sacred Scriptures approved for liturgical use in the territories for which the translation is being prepared. At the same time, care should be taken to avoid weighting down the text by clumsily over-elaborating the more delicate biblical allusions.

50. Since the liturgical books of the Roman Rite contain many fundamental words of the theological and spiritual tradition of the Roman Church, every effort must be made to preserve this system of vocabulary rather than substituting other words that are alien to the liturgical and catechetical usage of the people of God in a given cultural and ecclesial context. For this reason, the following principles in particular are to be observed:

a) In translating words of greater theological significance, an appropriate degree of coordination should be sought between the liturgical text and the authoritative vernacular translation of the Catechism of the Catholic Church, provided that such a translation exists or is being prepared, whether in the language in question or in a very closely related language;

b) Whenever it would be inappropriate to use the same vocabulary or the same expression in the liturgical text as in the Catechism, the translator should be solicitous to render fully the doctrinal and theological meaning of the terms and of the text itself;

c) One should maintain the vocabulary that has gradually developed in a given vernacular language to distinguish the individual liturgical ministers, vessels, furnishings, and vesture from similar persons or things pertaining to everyday life and usage; words that lack such a sacral character are not to be used instead;

d) In translating important words, due constancy is to be observed throughout the various parts of the Liturgy, with due regard for n. 53 below.

51. On the other hand, a variety of vocabulary in the original text should give rise, insofar as possible, to a corresponding variety in the translations. The translation may be weakened and made trite, for example, by the use of a single vernacular term for rendering differing Latin terms such as *satiari, sumere, vegetari,* and *pasci,* on the one hand, or the nouns *caritas* and *dilectio* on the other, or the words *anima, animus, cor, mens,* and *spiritus,* to give some examples. Similarly, a deficiency in translating the varying forms of addressing God, such as *Domine, Deus, Omnipotens aeterne Deus, Pater,* and so forth, as well as the various words expressing supplication, may render the translation monotonous and obscure the rich and beautiful way in which the relationship between the faithful and God is expressed in the Latin text.

52. The translator should strive to maintain the denotation, or primary sense of the words and expressions found in the original text, as well as their connotation, that is, the finer shades of meaning or emotion evoked by them, and thus to ensure that the text be open to other orders of meaning that may have been intended in the original text.

53. Whenever a particular Latin term has a rich meaning that is difficult to render into a modern language (such as the words *munus, famulus, consubstantialis, propitius,* etc.) various solutions may be employed in the translations, whether the term be translated by a single vernacular word or by several, or by the coining of a new word, or perhaps by the adaptation or transcription of the same term into a language or alphabet that is different from the original text (cf. above, n. 21), or the use of an already existing word which may bear various meanings.[37]

54. To be avoided in translations is any psychologizing tendency, especially a tendency to replace words treating of the theological virtues by others expressing merely human emotions. As regards words or expressions conveying a properly divine notion of causality (e.g., those expressed in Latin by the words *"praesta, ut . . ."*), one should avoid employing words or expressions denoting a merely extrinsic or profane sort of assistance instead.

55. Certain words that may appear to have been introduced into the Latin liturgical text for reasons of meter or other technical or literary reasons convey, in reality, a properly theological content, so that they are to be

preserved, insofar as possible, in the translation. It is necessary to translate with the utmost precision those words that express aspects of the mysteries of faith and the proper disposition of the Christian soul.

56. Certain expressions that belong to the heritage of the whole or of a great part of the ancient Church, as well as others that have become part of the general human patrimony, are to be respected by a translation that is as literal as possible, as for example the words of the people's response *Et cum spiritu tuo,* or the expression *mea culpa, mea culpa, mea maxima culpa* in the Act of Penance of the Order of Mass.

B. Syntax, style and literary genre

57. That notable feature of the Roman Rite, namely its straightforward, concise and compact manner of expression, is to be maintained insofar as possible in the translation. Furthermore, the same manner of rendering a given expression is to be maintained throughout the translation, insofar as feasible. These principles are to be observed:

a) The connection between various expressions, manifested by subordinate and relative clauses, the ordering of words, and various forms of parallelism, is to be maintained as completely as possible in a manner appropriate to the vernacular language.

b) In the translation of terms contained in the original text, the same person, number, and gender is to be maintained insofar as possible.

c) The theological significance of words expressing causality, purpose or consequence (such as *ut, ideo, enim,* and *quia*) is to be maintained, though different languages may employ varying means for doing so.

d) The principles set forth above, in n. 51, regarding variety of vocabulary, are to be observed also in the variety of syntax and style (for example, in the location within the Collect of the vocative addressed to God).

58. The literary and rhetorical genres of the various texts of the Roman Liturgy are to be maintained.[38]

59. Since liturgical texts by their very nature are intended to be proclaimed orally and to be heard in the liturgical celebration, they are characterized by a certain manner of expression that differs from that found in everyday speech or in texts intended be read silently. Examples of this include recurring and recognizable patterns of syntax and style, a solemn or exalted tone, alliteration and assonance, concrete and vivid images,

Translating Tradition

repetition, parallelism and contrast, a certain rhythm, and at times, the lyric of poetic compositions. If it is sometimes not possible to employ in the translation the same stylistic elements as in the original text (as often happens, for example, in the case of alliteration or assonance), even so, the translator should seek to ascertain the intended effect of such elements in the mind of the hearer as regards thematic content, the expression of contrast between elements, emphasis, and so forth. Then he should employ the full possibilities of the vernacular language skillfully in order to achieve as integrally as possible the same effect as regards not only the conceptual content itself, but the other aspects as well. In poetic texts, greater flexibility will be needed in translation in order to provide for the role played by the literary form itself in expressing the content of the texts. Even so, expressions that have a particular doctrinal or spiritual importance or those that are more widely known are, insofar as possible, to be translated literally.

60. A great part of the liturgical texts are composed with the intention of their being sung by the priest celebrant, the deacon, the cantor, the people, or the choir. For this reason, the texts should be translated in a manner that is suitable for being set to music. Still, in preparing the musical accompaniment, full account must be taken of the authority of the text itself. Whether it be a question of the texts of Sacred Scripture or of those taken from the Liturgy and already duly confirmed, paraphrases are not to be substituted with the intention of making them more easily set to music, nor may hymns considered generically equivalent be employed in their place.[39]

61. Texts that are intended to be sung are particularly important because they convey to the faithful a sense of the solemnity of the celebration, and manifest unity in faith and charity by means of a union of voices.[40] The hymns and canticles contained in the modern *editiones typicae* constitute a minimal part of the historic treasury of the Latin Church, and it is especially advantageous that they be preserved in the printed vernacular editions, even if placed there in addition to hymns composed originally in the vernacular language. The texts for singing that are composed originally in the vernacular language would best be drawn from Sacred Scripture or from the liturgical patrimony.

62. Certain liturgical texts of ecclesiastical composition are associated with ritual actions expressed by a particular posture, gesture, or the use of signs. Thus, in preparing appropriate translations it will be advantageous to consider such factors as the time required for reciting the words, their suitability for being sung or continually repeated, etc.

Appendix

4. Norms pertaining to special types of texts

A. The Eucharistic Prayers

63. The high point of all liturgical action is the celebration of the Mass, in which the Eucharistic Prayer or Anaphora in turn occupies a pre-eminent place.[41] For this reason, the approved translations of the approved Eucharistic Prayers require the utmost care, especially as regards the sacramental formulae, for which a particular procedure is prescribed below, in nn. 85-86.

64. Without real necessity, successive revisions of translations should not notably change the previously approved vernacular texts of the Eucharistic Prayers which the faithful will have committed gradually to memory. Whenever a completely new translation is necessary, the principles given below, in n. 74, are to be observed.

B. The Creed or Profession of Faith

65. By means of the Creed (*Symbolum*) or profession of faith, the whole gathered people of God respond to the word of God proclaimed in the Sacred Scriptures and expounded in the homily, recalling and confessing the great mysteries of the faith by means of a formula approved for liturgical use.[42] The Creed is to be translated according to the precise wording that the tradition of the Latin Church has bestowed upon it, including the use of the first person singular, by which is clearly made manifest that "the confession of faith is handed down in the Creed, as it were, as coming from the person of the whole Church, united by means of the Faith."[43] In addition, the expression *carnis resurrectionem* is to be translated literally wherever the Apostles' Creed is prescribed or may be used in the Liturgy.[44]

C. The "Praenotanda" and the texts of a rubrical or juridical nature

66. All parts of the various liturgical books are to be translated in the same order in which they are set forth in the Latin text of the *editio typica*, including the *institutiones generales*, the *praenotanda*, and the instructions supplied in the various rites, which function as a support for the whole structure of the Liturgy.[45] The distinction between the various liturgical roles and the designation of the liturgical ministers by their proper titles is to be maintained in the translation precisely as it is in the rubrics of the *editio typica*, maintaining due regard for the principles mentioned in n. 50c above.[46]

Translating Tradition

67. Wherever such *praenotanda* or other texts of the *editiones typicae* explicitly call for adaptations or specific applications to be introduced by the Conferences, as for example the parts of the Missal that are to be defined more specifically by the Conference of Bishops,[47] it is permissible to insert these prescriptions into the text, provided that they have received the *recognitio* of the Apostolic See. It is not required in such cases, by their very nature, to translate these parts verbatim as they stand in the *editio typica*. Nevertheless, a mention is to be made of the decree of approbation of the Conference of Bishops and of the *recognitio* granted by the Congregation for Divine Worship and the Discipline of the Sacraments.

68. At the beginning of the vernacular editions are to be placed the decrees by which the *editiones typicae* have been promulgated by the competent Dicastery of the Apostolic See, with due regard for the prescriptions found in n. 78. Also to be placed there are the decrees by means of which the *recognitio* of the Holy See has been granted for the translations, or at least the mention of the *recognitio* is to be made together with the date, month, year, and protocol number of the decree issued by the Dicastery. Since these are also historical documents, the names of the Dicasteries or other organ of the Apostolic See are to be translated exactly as they appeared on the date of promulgation of the document, rather than being altered to reflect the present name of the same or equivalent body.

69. The editions of the liturgical books prepared in the vernacular language are to correspond in every part to the titles, the ordering of texts, the rubrics, and the system of numbering that appears in the *editio typica*, unless otherwise directed in the *praenotanda* of the same books. Furthermore, any additions approved by the Congregation for Divine Worship and the Discipline of the Sacraments are to be inserted either in a supplement or appendix, or in their proper place in the book, as the Apostolic See shall have directed.

III
ON THE PREPARATION OF TRANSLATIONS
AND THE ESTABLISHMENT OF COMMISSIONS

1. THE MANNER OF PREPARING A TRANSLATION

70. On account of the entrusting to the Bishops of the task of preparing liturgical translations,[48] this work is committed in a particular way to the liturgical commission duly established by the Conference of Bishops.

Wherever such a commission is lacking, the task of preparing the translation is to be entrusted to two or three Bishops who are expert in liturgical, biblical, philological or musical studies.[49] As regards the examination and approbation of the texts, each individual Bishop must regard this duty as a direct, solemn and personal fiduciary responsibility.

71. In nations where many languages are used, the translations into individual vernacular languages are to be prepared and submitted to the special examination of those Bishops involved.[50] Nevertheless, it is the Conference of Bishops as such that retains the right and the power to posit all of those actions mentioned in this Instruction as pertaining to the Conference; thus, it pertains to the full Conference to approve a text and to submit it for the *recognitio* of the Apostolic See.

72. The Bishops, in fulfilling their mission of preparing translations of liturgical texts, are carefully to ensure that the translations be the fruit of a truly common effort rather than of any single person or of a small group of persons.

73. Whenever a Latin *editio typica* of a given liturgical book is promulgated, it is necessary that it be followed in a timely manner by the preparation of a translation of the same book, which the Conference of Bishops is to send, after having duly approved it, to the Congregation for Divine Worship and the Discipline of the Sacraments, to whom it pertains to grant the *recognitio* according to the norms set forth in this Instruction, and also in keeping with others established by the law.[51] However, when it is a question of a change affecting only a part of the Latin *editio typica* or the insertion of new elements, these new elements are to be maintained fully and faithfully in all succeeding editions produced in the vernacular language.

74. A certain stability ought to be maintained whenever possible in successive editions prepared in modern languages. The parts that are to be committed to memory by the people, especially if they are sung, are to be changed only for a just and considerable reason. Nevertheless, if more significant changes are necessary for the purpose of bringing the text into conformity with the norms contained in this Instruction, it will be preferable to make such changes at one time, rather than prolonging them over the course of several editions. In such case, a suitable period of catechesis should accompany the publication of the new text.

75. The translation of liturgical texts requires not only a rare degree of expertise, but also a spirit of prayer and of trust in the divine assistance

granted not only to the translators, but to the Church herself, throughout the whole process leading to the definitive approbation of the texts. The readiness to see one's own work examined and revised by others is an essential trait that should be evident in one who undertakes the translation of liturgical texts. Furthermore, all translations or texts prepared in vernacular languages, including those of the *praenotanda* and the rubrics, are to be anonymous with respect to persons as well as to institutions consisting of several persons, as in the case of the *editiones typicae*.[52]

76. In implementing the decisions of the Second Vatican Council, it has become evident from the mature experience of the nearly four decades of the liturgical renewal that have elapsed since the Council that the need for translations of liturgical texts — at least as regards the major languages — is experienced not only by the Bishops in governing the particular Churches, but also by the Apostolic See, for the effective exercise of her universal solicitude for the Christian faithful in the City of Rome and throughout the world. Indeed, in the Diocese of Rome, especially in many of the Churches and institutes of the City that depend in some way on the Diocese or the organs of the Holy See, as well as in the activity of the Dicasteries of the Roman Curia and the Pontifical Representations, the major languages are widely and frequently employed even in liturgical celebrations. For this reason, it has been determined that in the future, the Congregation for Divine Worship and the Discipline of the Sacraments will be involved more directly in the preparation of the translations into these major languages.

77. Furthermore, as regards the major languages, an integral translation of all of the liturgical books is to be prepared in a timely manner. Translations heretofore approved *ad interim* are to be perfected or thoroughly revised, as the case requires, and afterwards submitted to the Bishops for definitive approbation in accordance with the norms set forth in this Instruction. Finally, they are to be sent to the Congregation for Divine Worship and the Discipline of the Sacraments with a request for the *recognitio*.[53]

78. In the case of the less diffused languages that are approved for liturgical use, the larger or more important liturgical books, in particular, may be translated, according to pastoral necessity and with the consent of the Congregation for Divine Worship and the Discipline of the Sacraments. The individual books thus selected are to be translated integrally, in the manner described in n. 66 above. As for the decrees, the *institutio generalis*, the *praenotanda* and the instructions, it is permissible to print them in a language that is different from the one used in the celebration, but nevertheless intelligible to the priest or deacon celebrants in the same territory.

Appendix

It is permissible to print the Latin text of the decrees, either in addition to the translation or instead of it.

2. THE APPROBATION OF THE TRANSLATION AND THE PETITION FOR THE *RECOGNITIO* OF THE APOSTOLIC SEE

79. The approbation liturgical texts, whether definitive, on the one hand, or *ad interim* or *ad experimentum* on the other, must be made by decree. In order that this be legitimately executed, the following are to be observed:[54]

a) For the legitimate passage of decrees, a two-thirds vote by secret ballot is required on the part of all who enjoy the right to a deliberative vote of the Conference of Bishops.

b) All acts to be examined by the Apostolic See, prepared in duplicate, signed by the President and Secretary of the Conference, and duly affixed with its seal, are to be sent to the Congregation for Divine Worship and the Discipline of the Sacraments. In these acts are to be contained:

i) the names of the Bishops or of those equivalent in law who were present at the meeting,

ii) a *relatio* of the proceedings, which should contain the results of the voting for each individual decree, including the number in favor, the number opposed, and the number abstaining.

c) Two copies are to be sent of the liturgical texts prepared in the vernacular language; insofar as possible, the same text should be sent on computer diskette;

d) In the particular *relatio*, the following should be explained clearly:[55]

i) the process and criteria followed in the work of translation.

ii) a list of the persons participating at various stages in the work, together with a brief note describing the qualifications and expertise of each.

iii) any changes that may have been introduced in relation to the previous translation of the same edition of the liturgical book are to be indicated clearly, together with the reasons for making such changes;

iv) an indication of any changes with respect to the content of the Latin *editio typica* together with the reasons which they were necessary, and with a notation of the prior consent of the Apostolic See for the introduction of such changes.

80. The practice of seeking the *recognitio* from the Apostolic See for all translations of liturgical books[56] accords the necessary assurance of the authenticity of the translation and its correspondence with the original texts. This practice both expresses and effects a bond of communion between the successor of blessed Peter and his brothers in the Episcopate. Furthermore, this *recognitio* is not a mere formality, but is rather an exercise of the power of governance, which is absolutely necessary (in the absence of which the act of the Conference of Bishops entirely in no way attains legal force); and modifications — even substantial ones — may be introduced by means of it.[57] For this reason it is not permissible to publish, for the use of celebrants or for the general public, any liturgical texts that have been translated or recently composed, as long as the *recognitio* is lacking. Since the *lex orandi* must always be in harmony with the *lex credendi* and must manifest and support the faith of the Christian people, the liturgical translations will not be capable of being worthy of God without faithfully transmitting the wealth of Catholic doctrine from the original text into the vernacular version, in such a way that the sacred language is adapted to the dogmatic reality that it contains.[58] Furthermore, it is necessary to uphold the principle according to which each particular Church must be in accord with the universal Church not only as regards the doctrine of the Faith and the sacramental signs, but also as regards those practices universally received through Apostolic and continuous tradition.[59] For these reasons, the required *recognitio* of the Apostolic See is intended to ensure that the translations themselves, as well as any variations introduced into them, will not harm the unity of God's people, but will serve it instead.[60]

81. The *recognitio* granted by the Apostolic See is to be indicated in the printed editions together with the *concordat cum originali* signed by the chairman of the liturgical commission of the Conference of Bishops, as well as the *imprimatur* undersigned by the President of the same Conference.[61] Afterwards, two copies of each printed edition are to be sent to the Congregation for Divine Worship and the Discipline of the Sacraments.[62]

82. Any alteration of a liturgical book that has already been approved by the Conference of Bishops with the subsequent *recognitio* of the Apostolic See, as regards either the selection of texts from liturgical books already published or the changing of the arrangement of the texts, must be done according to the procedure established above, in n. 79, with due regard also for the prescriptions set forth in n. 22. Any other manner of

proceeding in particular circumstances may be employed only if it is authorized by the Statutes of the Conference of Bishops or equivalent legislation approved by the Apostolic See.[63]

83. As regards the editions of liturgical books prepared in vernacular languages, the approbation of the Conference of Bishops as well as the *recognitio* of the Apostolic See are to be regarded as valid only for the territory of the same Conference, so that these editions may not be used in another territory without the consent of the Apostolic See, except in those particular circumstances mentioned above, in nn. 18 and 76, and in keeping with the norms set forth there.

84. Wherever a certain Conference of Bishops lacks sufficient resources or instruments for the preparation and printing of a liturgical book, the President of the that Conference is to explain the situation to the Congregation for Divine Worship and the Discipline of the Sacraments, to whom it pertains to establish or to approve any different arrangement, such as the publication of liturgical books together with other Conferences or the use of those already employed elsewhere. Such a concession shall only be granted by the Holy See *ad actum*.

3. ON THE TRANSLATION AND APPROBATION OF SACRAMENTAL FORMULAE

85. As regards the translation of the sacramental formulae, which the Congregation for Divine Worship must submit to the judgment of the Supreme Pontiff, the following principles are to be observed besides those required for the translation of other liturgical texts:[64]

a) In the case of the English, French, German, Italian, Portuguese and Spanish languages, all of the acts are to be presented in that language;

b) If the translation differs from a vernacular text already prepared and approved in the same language, it is necessary to explain the reason for the introduction of the change;

c) The President and Secretary of the Conference of Bishops should testify that the translation has been approved by the Conference of Bishops.

86. In the case of the less widely diffused languages, everything shall be prepared as set forth above. The acts, however, are to be prepared with great care in one of the languages mentioned above as more widely known, rendering the meaning of each individual word of the vernacular language. The President and Secretary of the Conference of Bishops, after

any necessary consultation with trustworthy experts, are to testify to the authenticity of the translation.[65]

4. ON A UNIFIED VERSION OF THE LITURGICAL TEXTS

87. It is recommended that there be a single translation of the liturgical books for each vernacular language, brought about by means of coordination among the Bishops of those regions where the same language is spoken.[66] If this proves truly impossible because of the circumstances, the individual Conferences of Bishops, after consultation with the Holy See, may decide either to adapt a previously existing translation or to prepare a new one. In either case, the *recognitio* of their acts is to be sought from the Congregation for Divine Worship and the Discipline of the Sacraments.

88. In the case of the Order of Mass and those parts of the Sacred Liturgy that call for the direct participation of the people, a single translation should exist in a given language,[67] unless a different provision is made in individual cases.

89. Texts which are common to several Conferences, as mentioned above in nn. 87-88, are ordinarily to be approved by each of the individual Conferences of Bishops which must use them, before the confirmation of the texts is granted by the Apostolic See.[68]

90. With due regard for Catholic traditions and for all of the principles and norms contained in this Instruction, an appropriate relationship or coordination is greatly to be desired, whenever possible, between any translations intended for common use in the various Rites of the Catholic Church, especially as regards the text of Sacred Scripture. The Bishops of the Latin Church are to foster the same in a spirit of respectful and fraternal cooperation.

91. A similar agreement is desirable also with the particular non-Catholic Eastern Churches or with the authorities of the Protestant ecclesial communities,[69] provided that it is not a question of a liturgical text pertaining to doctrinal matters still in dispute, and provided also that the Churches or ecclesial communities involved have a sufficient number of adherents and that those consulted are truly capable of functioning as representatives of the same ecclesial communities. In order completely to avoid the danger of scandal or of confusion among the Christian faithful, the Catholic Church must retain full liberty of action in such agreements, even in civil law.

Appendix

92. So that there might be unity in the liturgical books even as regards vernacular translations, and so that the resources and the efforts of the Church might not be consumed needlessly, the Apostolic See has promoted, among other possible solutions, the establishment of "mixed" commissions, that is, those in whose work several Conferences of Bishops participate.[70]

93. The Congregation for Divine Worship and the Discipline of the Sacraments erects such "mixed" commissions at the request of the Conferences of Bishops involved; afterwards the commission is governed by statutes approved by the Apostolic See.[71] It is ordinarily to be hoped that each and every one of the Conferences of Bishops will have deliberated the matter of the above-mentioned establishment of the commission as well as of the composition of its statutes before the petition is submitted to the Congregation for Divine Worship and the Discipline of the Sacraments. Even so, if it is judged opportune by that Dicastery due to the great number of Conferences, or the protracted period of time required for a vote, or particular pastoral necessity, it is not excluded that the statutes be prepared and approved by the same Dicastery, after consultation, insofar as possible, with at least some of the Bishops involved.

94. A "mixed" commission, by its very nature, provides assistance to the Bishops rather than substituting for them as regards their pastoral mission and their relations with the Apostolic See.[72] For a "mixed" commission does not constitute a *tertium quid* place between the Conferences of Bishops and the Holy See, nor is it to be regarded as a means of communication between them. The Members of the Commission are always Bishops, or at least those equivalent in law to Bishops. It pertains to the Bishops, furthermore, to direct the Commission as its Members.

95. It would be advantageous that among the Bishops who participate in the work of each "mixed" commission, there be at least some who are responsible for dealing with liturgical matters in their respective Conferences, as, for example, the chairman of the liturgical commission of the Conference.

96. Such a commission, in fact, insofar as possible, should exercise its office by means of the resources of the liturgical commissions of the individual Conferences involved, using their experts, their technical resources, and their secretarial staff. For example, the work undertaken is coordinated in such a way that a first draft of the translation is prepared

Translating Tradition

by the liturgical commission of one Conference and then improved by the other Conferences, even in light of the diversity of expression prevailing in the same language in the individual territories.

97. It is preferable that at least some Bishops participate at the various stages of work on a given text, until the time when the mature text is submitted to the Plenary Assembly of the Conference of Bishops for its examination and approval and is then sent immediately by the Conference President, with the signature also of the Secretary General, to the Apostolic See for the *recognitio.*

98. In addition, the "mixed" commissions are to limit themselves to the translation of the *editiones typicae,* leaving aside all theoretical questions not directly related to this work, and not involving themselves either in relations with other "mixed" commissions or in the composition of original texts.

99. In fact, the necessity remains for establishing commissions dealing with the Sacred Liturgy as well as sacred art and sacred music according to the norm of law in each diocese and territory of the Conference of Bishops.[73] These commissions shall work in their own right for the purposes proper to them, and shall not cede the matters entrusted to them to any "mixed" commission.

100. All of the principal collaborators of any "mixed" commission who are not Bishops, and to whom a stable mission is entrusted by such commissions, require the *nihil obstat* granted by the Congregation for Divine Worship and the Discipline of the Sacraments before beginning their work. The *nihil obstat* will be granted after consideration of their academic degrees and testimonies regarding their expertise, and a letter of recommendation submitted by their own diocesan Bishop. In the preparation of the statutes mentioned above, in n. 93, the manner in which the request for the *nihil obstat* is to be made shall be described with greater precision.

101. All, including the experts, are to conduct their work anonymously, observing confidentiality to which all who are not Bishops are to be bound by contract.

102. It is also advantageous that the terms of office of the members, collaborators and experts be renewed periodically in a manner defined by the Statutes. On account of a need on the part of the Commissions that may become evident in the course of the work, the Congregation for Divine Worship and the Discipline of the Sacraments may grant, upon request,

a prolongation by indult of the term of office established for a particular member, collaborator or expert.

103. In the case of previously existing "mixed" Commissions, their statutes are to be revised within two years from the date that this Instruction enters into force, according to the norms of n. 93 and of the other norms prescribed by this Instruction.

104. For the good of the faithful, the Holy See reserves to itself the right to prepare translations in any language, and to approve them for liturgical use.[74] Nevertheless, even if the Apostolic See, by means of the Congregation for Divine Worship and the Discipline of the Sacraments, may intervene from time to time out of necessity in the preparation of translations, it still belongs to the competent Conference of Bishops to approve their assumption into liturgical use within the boundaries of a given ecclesiastical territory, unless otherwise explicitly indicated in the decree of approbation of the translation promulgated by the Apostolic See. Afterwards, for the purpose of obtaining the *recognitio* of the Holy See, the Conference shall transmit the decree of approbation for its territory together with the text itself, in accordance with the norms of this Instruction and of the other requirements of the law.

105. For reasons such as those set forth in nn. 76 and 84 above or for other urgent reasons of pastoral need, commissions, councils, committees, or work groups depending directly on the Apostolic See are established by decree of the Congregation for Divine Worship and the Discipline of the Sacraments for the purpose of working on the translation either of individual liturgical books or of several. In this case, insofar as possible, at least some of the Bishops involved in the matter will be consulted.

6. THE COMPOSITION OF NEW LITURGICAL TEXTS IN A VERNACULAR LANGUAGE

106. Regarding the composition of new liturgical texts prepared in vernacular languages, which may perhaps be added to those translated from the Latin *editiones typicae*, the norms currently in force are to be observed, in particular those contained in the Instruction *Varietates legitimae*.[75] An individual Conference of Bishops shall establish one or more Commissions for the preparation of texts or for the work involved in the suitable adaptation of texts. The texts are then to be sent to the Congregation for Divine Worship and the Discipline of the Sacraments for the *recognitio*, prior to the publication of any books intended for the celebrants or for the general use of the Christian faithful.[76]

Translating Tradition

107. It is to be borne in mind that the composition of new texts of prayers or rubrics is not an end in itself, but must be undertaken for the purpose of meeting a particular cultural or pastoral need. For this reason it is strictly the task of the local and national liturgical Commissions, and not of the Commissions treated in nn. 92-104 above. New texts composed in a vernacular language, just as the other adaptations legitimately introduced, are to contain nothing that is inconsistent with the function, meaning, structure, style, theological content, traditional vocabulary or other important qualities of the texts found in the *editiones typicae*.[77]

108. Sung texts and liturgical hymns have a particular importance and efficacy. Especially on Sunday, the "Day of the Lord," the singing of the faithful gathered for the celebration of Holy Mass, no less than the prayers, the readings and the homily, express in an authentic way the message of the Liturgy while fostering a sense of common faith and communion in charity.[78] If they are used widely by the faithful, they should remain relatively fixed so that confusion among the people may be avoided. Within five years from the publication of this Instruction, the Conferences of Bishops, necessarily in collaboration with the national and diocesan Commissions and with other experts, shall provide for the publication of a directory or repertory of texts intended for liturgical singing. This document shall be transmitted for the necessary *recognitio* to the Congregation for Divine Worship and the Discipline of the Sacraments.

IV
THE PUBLICATION OF LITURGICAL BOOKS

109. Of the liturgical books of the Roman Rite containing only Latin texts, only the one published by decree of the Congregation having competency at the time is designated the *"editio typica."*[79] The *editiones typicae* published prior to this Instruction were issued either *Typis Polyglottis Vaticanis* or by the *Libreria Editrice Vaticana;* in the future, they are usually to be printed by the *Tipografia Vaticana,* while the right of publication is reserved to the *Libreria Editrice Vaticana.*

110. The norms of this Instruction, as regards all rights, refer to the *editiones typicae* that have been or will be published, whether of a whole book or of a part: namely, the editions of the *Missale Romanum,* the *Ordo Missae,* the Lectionary of the *Missale Romanum,* the Evangeliary of the *Missale Romanum,* the *Missale parvum* extracted from the *Missale Romanum* and *Lectionarium,* the *Passio Domini Nostri Iesu Christi,* the *Liturgia Horarum,* the

Rituale Romanum, the *Pontificale Romanum*, the *Martyrologium Romanum*, the *Collectio Missarum de Beata Maria Virgine* and its Lectionary, the *Graduale Romanum*, the *Antiphonale Romanum*, as well as the other books of Gregorian chant and the editions of the books of the Roman Rite promulgated by decree as *editiones typicae*, such as the *Caeremoniale Episcoporum* and the *Calendarium Romanum*.

111. As regards the liturgical books of the Roman Rite promulgated in an *editio typica* either before or after the Second Vatican Council by decree of the Congregations competent at the time, the Apostolic See, through the *Administratio Patrimonii* or, in its name and by its mandate, through the *Libreria Editrice Vaticana*, possesses and reserves to itself the right of ownership commonly known as "copyright." The granting of permission for a reprinting pertains to the Congregation for Divine Worship and the Discipline of the Sacraments.

112. Of the liturgical books of the Roman Rite, those prepared in the Latin language by an editor after the publication of the *editio typica*, with the permission of the Congregation for Divine Worship and the Discipline of the Sacraments, are said to be *"iuxta typicam."*

113. As regards the editions *iuxta typicam* intended for liturgical use: the right of printing liturgical books containing only the Latin text is reserved to the *Libreria Editrice Vaticana* and to those editors to whom the Congregation for Divine Worship and the Discipline of the Sacraments will have chosen to grant contracts, unless a different provision is made in the norms inserted into the *editio typica* itself.

114. The right of translating the liturgical books of the Roman Rite in a vernacular language, or at least the right of approving them for liturgical use and of printing and publishing them in their own territory, remains uniquely that of the Conference of Bishops, with due regard, however, to the rights of *recognitio*[80] and the proprietary rights of the Apostolic See, also set forth in this Instruction.

115. As regards the publication of liturgical books translated into the vernacular which are the property of a given Conference of Bishops, the right of publication is reserved to those editors to whom the Conference of Bishops shall have given this right by contract, with due regard for the requirements both of civil law and of juridical custom prevailing in each country for the publication of books.

116. In order for an editor to be able to proceed to the printing of editions *iuxta typicam* intended for liturgical use, he must do the following:

a) in the case of books containing only the Latin text, obtain, in each single instance, the consent of the Congregation for Divine Worship and the Discipline of the Sacraments, and then enter into an agreement with the *Administratio Patrimonii Sedis Apostolicae* or with the *Libreria Editrice Vaticana*, which acts in the name and by the mandate of the same body, regarding the conditions for the publication of such books;

b) in the case of books containing texts in a vernacular language, obtain the consent, according to the circumstances, of the President of the Conference of Bishops, the Institute or the Commission that manages the matter in the name of several Conferences by license of the Holy See, and enter at the same time into an agreement with this body regarding the conditions for publication of such books, with due regard for the norms and laws in force in that country;

c) in the case of books containing principally a vernacular text but also containing extensive use of the Latin text, the norms of n. 116a are to be observed for the Latin part.

117. The rights of publication and the copyright for all translations of liturgical books, or at least the rights in civil law necessary for exercising complete liberty in publishing or correcting texts, is to remain with the Conferences of Bishops or their national liturgical Commissions.[81] The same body shall possess the right of taking any measures necessary to prevent or correct any improper use of the texts.

118. Wherever the copyright for translated liturgical texts is common to several Conferences, a licensing agreement is to be prepared for the individual Conferences, such that, insofar as possible, the matter may be administrated by the individual Conferences themselves, according to the norm of law. Otherwise, a body shall be established for such administration by the Apostolic See, after consultation with the Bishops.

119. The correspondence of the liturgical books with the *editiones typicae* approved for liturgical use, in the case of a text prepared only in the Latin language, must be established by the attestation of the Congregation for Divine Worship and the Discipline of the Sacraments; however, in the case of a text prepared in a vernacular language or in the case described above, in n. 116 c, it must be established by attestation of the local Ordinary in whose diocese the books are published.[82]

120. The books from which the liturgical texts are recited in the vernacular with or on behalf of the people should be marked by such a dignity that

the exterior appearance of the book itself will lead the faithful to a greater reverence for the word of God and for sacred realities.[83] Thus it is necessary as soon as possible to move beyond the temporary phase characterized by leaflets or fascicles, wherever these exist. All books intended for the liturgical use of priest or deacon celebrants are to be of a size sufficient to distinguish them from the books intended for the personal use of the faithful. To be avoided in them is any extravagance which would necessarily lead to costs that would be unaffordable for some. Pictures or images on the cover and in the pages of the book should be characterized by a certain noble simplicity and by the use of only those styles that have a universal and perennial appeal in the cultural context.

121. Even in the case of pastoral aids published for the private use of the faithful and intended to foster their participation in the liturgical celebrations, the publishers must observe the proprietary rights:

a) of the Holy See, in the case of the Latin text, or of the Gregorian music in books of chant published either before or after the Second Vatican Council — with the exception, however, of those rights conceded universally, or those to be thus conceded in the future;

b) of the Conference of Bishops or of several Conferences of Bishops simultaneously, in the case of a text prepared in a vernacular language or of the music printed in the same text, which is the property of the Conference or Conferences.

For these aids, especially if published in the form of books, the consent of the diocesan Bishop is required, according to the norm of law.[84]

122. Care is to be taken to ensure that the choice of publishers for the printing of the liturgical books be made in such a way as to exclude any whose publications are not readily seen to conform to the spirit and norms of Catholic tradition.

123. Regarding texts produced by agreement with the particular Churches and ecclesial communities separated from the communion of the Holy See, it is necessary that the Catholic Bishops and the Apostolic See retain full rights for introducing any changes or corrections that may be deemed necessary for their use among Catholics.

124. According to the judgment of the Conference of Bishops, leaflets or cards containing liturgical texts for the use of the faithful may be excepted from the general rule by which liturgical books prepared in a vernacular

language must contain everything that is in the Latin *textus typicus* or *editio typica*. As for the official editions, namely those for the liturgical use of the priest, deacon or competent lay minister, the norms mentioned above, in nn. 66-69, are to be maintained.[85]

125. Besides what is contained in the *editio typica* or foreseen or set forth specifically in this Instruction, no text is to be added in the vernacular edition without prior approbation granted by the Congregation for Divine Worship and the Discipline of the Sacraments.

V
THE TRANSLATION OF PROPER LITURGICAL TEXTS

1. DIOCESAN PROPERS

126. In the preparation of a translation of texts of a diocesan liturgical approved by the Apostolic See as *textus typici,* the following are to be observed:

a) The translation is to be done by the diocesan liturgical Commission[86] or by another body designated by the diocesan Bishop for this purpose, and then it must be approved by the diocesan Bishop, after consultation with his clergy and with experts;

b) The translation is to be sent to the Congregation for Divine Worship and the Discipline of the Sacraments for the *recognitio*, along with three copies of the *textus typicus* together with the translation;

c) A *relatio* is to be prepared as well, which is to contain:

i) the decree by which the *textus typicus* has been approved by the Apostolic See,

ii) the process and criteria followed in the translation;

iii) a list of the persons who have participated at various stages of the work, together with a brief description of their experience or abilities, and of their academic degrees;

d) In the case of the less widely diffused languages, the Conference of Bishops should testify that the text is accurately translated into the language in question, as mentioned above, in n. 86.

Appendix

127. In the printed text are to be contained the decrees by means of which the *recognitio* of the Holy See is granted for the translations; or at least a mention is to be made of the *recognitio*, including the date, the month, the year, and the protocol number of the decree published by the Dicastery, in keeping with the same norms as above, in n. 68. Two copies of the printed text are to be sent to the Congregation for Divine Worship and the Discipline of the Sacraments.

2. PROPERS OF RELIGIOUS FAMILIES

128. In the preparation the translation of texts approved by the Apostolic See as *textus typici* for religious families, that is, Institutes of Consecrated Life or Societies of Apostolic Life, or other approved associations or organizations having the rights to their use, the following are to be observed:

a) The translation is to be made by the general liturgical Commission or by another body constituted for the purpose by the Supreme Moderator or at least by his mandate given to the Provincial Superior, and then it is to be approved by the Supreme Moderator with the deliberative vote of his Council, after any necessary consultation with experts and with appropriate members of the Institute or Society;

b) The translation is to be sent to the Congregation for Divine Worship and the Discipline of the Sacraments for the *recognitio*, together with three copies of the *textus typicus*;

c) A *relatio* is also to be prepared, which is to contain:

> i) the decree by which the *textus typicus* has been approved by the Apostolic See,

> ii) the process and criteria followed in the translation,

> iii) a list of the persons who have participated at various stages of the work, together with a brief description of their experience or abilities, and of their academic degrees;

d) In the case of the less widely diffused languages, the Conference of Bishops should testify that the text is accurately translated into the language in question, as mentioned above, in n. 86.

e) As regards religious families of diocesan right, the same procedure is to be followed, but in addition, the text is to be sent by the diocesan Bishop, together with his judgment of approbation, to the Congregation for Divine Worship and the Discipline of the Sacraments.

129. In the liturgical Propers of religious families, the translation of the Sacred Scriptures to be employed for liturgical use is to be the same one approved for liturgical use according to the norm of law for the same territory. If this proves difficult, the matter is to be referred to the Congregation for Divine Worship and the Discipline of the Sacraments.

130. In the printed text are to be contained the decrees by means of which the *recognitio* of the Holy See is granted for the translations, or at least a mention is to be made of the *recognitio*, including the date, the month, the year, and the protocol number of the decree published by the Dicastery, in keeping with the same norms as above, in n. 68. Two copies of the printed text are to be sent to the Congregation for Divine Worship and the Discipline of the Sacraments.

CONCLUSION

131. Approbation granted in the past for individual liturgical translations remains in effect even if a principle or criterion has been followed which differs from those contained in this Instruction. Nevertheless, from the day on which this Instruction is published, a new period begins for the making of emendations or for undertaking anew the consideration of the introduction of vernacular languages or idioms into liturgical use, as well as for revising translations heretofore made into vernacular languages.

132. Within five years from the date of publication of this Instruction, the Presidents of the Conferences of Bishops and the Supreme Moderators of religious families and institutes equivalent in law are bound to present to the Congregation for Divine Worship and the Discipline of the Sacraments an integral plan regarding the liturgical books translated into the vernacular in their respective territories or institutes.

133. In addition, the norms established by this Instruction attain full force for the emendation of previous translations, and any further delay in making such emendations is to be avoided. It is to be hoped that this new effort will provide stability in the life of the Church, so as to lay a firm foundation for supporting the liturgical life of God's people and bringing about a solid renewal of catechesis.

Appendix

*After the preparation of this Instruction by the Congregation for Divine Worship
and the Discipline of the Sacraments in virtue of the mandate of the Supreme
Pontiff transmitted in a letter of the Cardinal Secretary of State dated 1 February
1997 (Prot. n. 408.304), the same Supreme Pontiff, in an audience granted to the
Cardinal Secretary of State on 20 March 2001, approved this Instruction and
confirmed it by his own authority, ordering that it be published, and that it enter
into force on the 25th day of April of the same year.*

*From the offices of the Congregation for Divine Worship and the Discipline of the
Sacraments, 28 March, the year 2001.*

Jorge A. Card. MEDINA ESTÉVEZ
Prefect

Francesco Pio TAMBURRINO
Archbishop Secretary

---

[1] SECOND VATICAN COUNCIL, Const. on the Sacred Liturgy *Sacrosanctum Concilium*,
nn. 1, 14, 21, 33; cf. COUNCIL OF TRENT, Sess. XXII, 17 September 1562, Doctr. *De ss.
Missae sacrif.*, c. 8 : Denz.-Schönm. n. 1749.

[2] The notion of the act of rendering a given text into another language is often
expressed in Latin by the words *versio, conversio, interpretatio, redditio,* and even
mutatio, transductio or similar words. Such is also the case in the Constitution
Sacrosanctum Concilium and many other recent documents of the Holy See.
Nevertheless, the sense often attributed to these terms in modern languages
involves some variation or discrepancy from the original text and its meaning.
For the purpose of excluding any ambiguity in this Instruction, which treats
explicitly of the same theme, the word *translatio,* with its cognates, has been
preferred. Even if their use presents some difficulty as regards Latin style or is
redolent of a "neologism," such terms nevertheless have a certain international
character and are able to communicate the present intent of the Apostolic See,
as they are able to be employed in many languages without the danger of error.

[3] Cf. S. CONGR. FOR DIVINE WORSHIP, Letter to the Presidents of the Conferences
of Bishops *De linguis vulgaribus in S. Liturgiam inducendis,* 5 June 1976: *Notitiae* 12
(1976) 300–302.

[4] Cf. SECOND VATICAN COUNCIL, Decr. On Eastern Catholic Churches, *Orientalium
Ecclesiarum,* n. 1.

Translating Tradition

[5] Cf. Second Vatican Council, Const. *Sacrosanctum Concilium,* n. 4; Decr. *Orientalium Ecclesiarum,* nn. 2, 6.

[6] Cf. Second Vatican Council, Const. *Sacrosanctum Concilium,* n. 38; Pope Paul VI, Apost. Const. *Missale Romanum:* AAS 61 (1969) 217–222. Cf. Missale Romanum, editio typica tertia: *Institutio Generalis,* n. 399.

[7] Congr. for Divine Worship and the Discipline of the Sacraments, Instr. IV "for the right implementation of the Second Vatican Council's Constitution on the Sacred Liturgy," *Varietates legitimae,* n. 17: AAS 87 (1995) 294–295; Missale Romanum, editio typica tertia: *Institutio Generalis,* n. 397.

[8] Second Vatican Council, Const. *Sacrosanctum Concilium,* n. 38; Missale Romanum, editio typica tertia: *Institutio Generalis,* n. 397.

[9] Pope Paul VI, Address to the Consilium "for the implementation of the Constitution on the Sacred Liturgy," 14 October 1968: AAS 60 (1968) 736.

[10] Cf. Congr. for Divine Worship and the Discipline of the Sacraments, Instr. *Varietates legitimae,* n. 36: AAS 87 (1995) 302; cf. also Missale Romanum, editio typica tertia: *Institutio Generalis,* n. 398.

[11] Cf. Pope John Paul II, Apost. Letter *Vicesimus quintus annus,* 4 December 1988, n. 20: AAS 81 (1989) 916.

[12] Cf. Pope Paul VI, Address to translators of liturgical texts into vernacular languages, 10 November 1965: AAS 57 (1965) 968.

[13] Congr. for Divine Worship and the Discipline of the Sacraments, Instr. *Varietates legitimae:* AAS 87 (1995) 288-314.

[14] S. Congr. for the Sacraments and Divine Worship, Letter to the Presidents of the Conferences of Bishops, *De linguis vulgaribus in S. Liturgiam inducendis,* 5 June 1976: *Notitiae* 12 (1976) 300–301.

[15] Cf. Second Vatican Council, Const. *Sacrosanctum Concilium,* n. 36 § 3; S. Congr. for the Sacraments and Divine Worship, Letter to the Presidents of the Conferences of Bishops *De linguis vulgaribus in S. Liturgiam inducendis,* 5 June 1976: *Notitiae* 12 (1976) 300–301.

[16] Cf. Second Vatican Council, Const. *Sacrosanctum Concilium,* n. 36 § 3; Pope Paul VI, Apost. Letter *Sacram Liturgiam,* 25 January 1964: AAS 56 (1964) 143; S. Congr. of Rites, Inst. *Inter Oecumenici,* 26 September 1964, nn. 27-29: AAS 56 (1964) 883; cf. S. Congr. for the Sacraments and Divine Worship, letter to the Presidents of the Conferences of Bishops *De linguis vulgaribus in S. Liturgiam inducendis,* 5 June 1976: *Notitiae* 12 (1976) 300–302.

[17] Cf., for example, Congr. for Divine Worship and the Discipline of the Sacraments, *Normae de celebranda Missa in «esperanto»,* 20 March 1990: *Notitiae* 26 (1990) 693–694.

[18] Cf. S. Congr. of Rites, Instr. *Inter Oecumenici,* n. 41: AAS 56 (1964) 886.

[19] Cf. Second Vatican Council, Const. *Sacrosanctum Concilium,* n. 33; Dogm. Const. on Divine Revelation, *Dei Verbum,* n. 8; cf. Missale Romanum, editio typica tertia: *Institutio Generalis,* n. 2.

[20] Cf. the Consilium "for the implementation of the Constitution on the Sacred Liturgy," Letter to the Presidents of the Conferences of Bishops, 21 June 1967: *Notitiae* 3 (1967) 296; Card. Secr. of State, Letter to the Pro-Prefect of the Congr. for Divine Worship and the Discipline of the Sacraments, 1 February 1997.

Appendix

[21] Cf. CONGR. FOR DIVINE WORSHIP AND THE DISCIPLINE OF THE SACRAMENTS, Instr., *Varietates legitimae*, 25 January 1994, n. 53: AAS 87 (1995) 308.

[22] *Ibid.*, n. 39: AAS 87 (1995) 303.

[23] *Ibid.*: AAS 87 (1995) 288–314; cf. MISSALE ROMANUM, editio typica tertia, *Institutio Generalis*, n. 397.

[24] Cf. S. CONGR. OF RITES, Instr. *Inter Oecumenici*, n. 40 a: AAS 56 (1964) 885.

[25] Cf. POPE PAUL VI, Address to translators of liturgical texts into vernacular languages, 10 November 1965: AAS 57 (1965) 968; CONGR. FOR DIVINE WORSHIP AND THE DISCIPLINE OF THE SACRAMENTS, Instr. *Varietates legitimae*, n. 53: AAS 87 (1995) 308.

[26] Cf. POPE JOHN PAUL II, Address to a group of Bishops from the United States of America on their *Ad limina* visit, 4 December 1993, n. 2: AAS 86 (1994) 755–756.

[27] Cf. SECOND VATICAN COUNCIL, Const. *Sacrosanctum Concilium*, n. 33.

[28] Cf., *ibid.*, n. 116; S. CONGR. OF RITES, Instr. *Musicam sacram*, 5 March 1967, n. 50: AAS 59 (1967) 314; S. CONGR. FOR DIVINE WORSHIP, Letter sent to the Bishops with the volume *Iubilate Deo*, 14 April 1974: *Notitiae* 10 (1974) 123–124; POPE JOHN PAUL II, Letter *Dominicae Cenae*, 24 February 1980, n. 10: AAS 72 (1980) 135; Address to a group of Bishops from the United States of America on their *Ad limina* visit, 9 October 1998, n. 3: AAS 91 (1999) 353-354; cf. MISSALE ROMANUM, editio typica tertia, *Institutio Generalis*, n. 41.

[29] Cf. SECOND VATICAN COUNCIL, Const. *Sacrosanctum Concilium*, n. 35, 52; S. CONGR. OF RITES, Instr. *Inter Oecumenici*, n. 54: AAS 56 (1964) 890; cf. POPE JOHN PAUL II, Apost. Exhortation *Catechesi tradendae*, 16 October 1979, n. 48: AAS 71 (1979) 1316; MISSALE ROMANUM, editio typica tertia: *Institutio Generalis*, n. 65.

[30] Cf., SECOND VATICAN COUNCIL, Decr. on Ecumenism, *Unitatis redintegratio;* Decl. on the Relationship of the Church to Non-Christian Religions, *Nostra aetate.*

[31] Cf. POPE PAUL VI, Apost. Const. *Laudis canticum*, 1 November 1970. n. 8: AAS 63 (1971) 532–533; OFFICIUM DIVINUM, Liturgia Horarum iuxta Ritum romanum, editio typica altera 1985: *Institutio Generalis de Liturgia Horarum*, n. 100; POPE JOHN PAUL II, Apost. Letter *Vicesimus quintus annus*, n. 8 : AAS 81 (1989) 904–905.

[32] Cf. COUNCIL OF TRENT, Session IV, 8 April 1546, *De libris sacris et de traditionibus recipiendis*, and *De vulgata editione Bibliorum et de modo interpretandi s. Scripturarum:* Denz.–Schönm., nn. 1501-1508 ; POPE JOHN PAUL II, Apost. Const. *Scripturarum thesaurus*, 25 April 1979: AAS 71 (1979) 558-559.

[33] Cf. POPE PAUL VI, Address to the Cardinals and Prelates of the Roman Curia, 23 December 1966, n. 11: AAS 59 (1967) 53–54; cf. Address to the Cardinals and Prelates of the Roman Curia, 22 December 1977: AAS 70 (1978) 43; cf. POPE JOHN PAUL II, Apost. Const. *Scripturarum thesaurus*, 25 April 1979: AAS 71 (1979) 558; *Nova Vulgata Bibliorum Sacrorum*, editio typica altera 1986, Praefatio ad Lectorem.

[34] Cf. OFFICIUM DIVINUM, Liturgia Horarum iuxta Ritum romanum, editio typica altera 1985: *Institutio Generalis de Liturgia Horarum*, nn. 100-109.

[35] SECOND VATICAN COUNCIL, Const. *Dei Verbum*, n. 22.

[36] Cf. POPE PAUL VI, Apost. Exhortation *Marialis cultus*, 11 February 1974, n. 30: AAS 66 (1974) 141–142.

[37] Cf. CONGR. FOR DIVINE WORSHIP AND THE DISCIPLINE OF THE SACRAMENTS, Instr. *Varietates legitimae*, n. 53: AAS 87 (1995) 308.

[38] Cf. *ibid.;* cf. MISSALE ROMANUM, editio typica tertia: *Institutio Generalis*, n. 392.

Translating Tradition

[39] Cf. MISSALE ROMANUM, editio typica tertia: *Institutio Generalis*, nn. 53, 57.

[40] Cf. POPE JOHN PAUL II, Apost. Letter *Dies Domini*, n. 50: AAS 90 (1998) 745.

[41] MISSALE ROMANUM, editio typica tertia: *Institutio Generalis*, n. 78.

[42] Cf. *ibid.*, n. 67.

[43] ST. THOMAS AQUINAS, *Summa Theologiae*, IIaIIae, I, 9.

[44] Cf. S. CONGR. FOR THE DOCTRINE OF THE FAITH, *Communicatio*, 2 December 1983: *Notitiae* 20 (1984) 181.

[45] Cf. SECOND VATICAN COUNCIL, Const. *Sacrosanctum Concilium*, n. 63b; S. CONGR. FOR DIVINE WORSHIP, Decl. *De interpretationibus popularibus novorum textuum liturgicorum*, 15 September 1969: *Notitiae* 5 (1969) 333–334.

[46] Cf. CONGR. FOR THE CLERGY et al., Instr. *Ecclesiae de mysterio*, 15 August 1997, art. 1-3, 6-12: AAS 89 (1997) 861–865, 869–874.

[47] Cf. MISSALE ROMANUM, editio typica tertia: *Institutio Generalis*, n. 389.

[48] Cf. SECOND VATICAN COUNCIL, Const. *Sacrosanctum Concilium*, n. 36; cf. *Code of Canon Law*, can 838 § 3.

[49] Cf. SECOND VATICAN COUNCIL, Const. *Sacrosanctum Concilium*, n. 44; S. CONGR. OF RITES, Instr. *Inter Oecumenici*, nn. 40 b, 44: AAS (1964) 885–886.

[50] Cf. S. CONGR. OF RITES, Instr. *Inter Oecumenici*, n. 40 d: AAS 56 (1964) 886.

[51] Cf., *Code of Canon Law*, can. 838.

[52] Cf. S. CONGR. FOR DIVINE WORSHIP, Decl., 15 May 1970: *Notitiae* 6 (1970) 153.

[53] Cf. POPE JOHN PAUL II, Apost. Letter *Vicesimus quintus annus*, n. 20: AAS 81 (1989) 916.

[54] Cf. SECOND VATICAN COUNCIL, Const. *Sacrosanctum Concilium*, n. 36; POPE PAUL VI, Apost. Letter *Sacram Liturgiam*, IX: AAS 56 (1964) 143; S. CONGR. OF RITES, Instr. *Inter Oecumenici*, nn. 27-29: AAS 56 (1964) 883; CENTR. COMM. FOR COORDINATING POST-CONCILIAR WORKS AND INTERPRETING THE DECREES OF THE COUNCIL, Response to Dubium: AAS 60 (1968) 361; cf. S. CONGR. FOR THE SACRAMENTS AND DIVINE WORSHIP, Letter to the Presidents of the Conferences of Bishops *De linguis vulgaribus in S. Liturgiam inducendis*, 5 June 1976: *Notitiae* 12 (1976) 300–302.

[55] Cf. S. CONGR. OF RITES, Instr. *Inter Oecumenici*, n. 30: AAS 56 (1964) 883; S. CONGR. FOR THE SACRAMENTS AND DIVINE WORSHIP, Letter to the Presidents of the Conferences of Bishops *De linguis vulgaribus in S. Liturgiam inducendis*, 5 June 1976: *Notitiae* 12 (1976) 302.

[56] Cf. SECOND VATICAN COUNCIL, Const. *Sacrosanctum Concilium*, n. 36; S. CONGR. OF RITES, Instr. *Inter Oecumenici*, nn. 20-21, 31: AAS (1964) 882, 884; *Code of Canon Law*, can. 838.

[57] Cf. PONT. COMM. FOR THE REVISION OF THE CODE OF CANON LAW, Acta: *Communicationes* 15 (1983) 173.

[58] Cf. POPE PAUL VI, Address to the Members and Experts of the Consilium "for the implementation of the Constitution on the Sacred Liturgy," 13 October 1966: AAS 58 (1966) 1146; Address to the Members and Experts of the Consilium "for the implementation of the Constitution on the Sacred Liturgy" 14 October 1968: AAS 60 (1968) 734.

[59] MISSALE ROMANUM, editio typica tertia, *Institutio Generalis*, n. 397.

[60] Cf. SECOND VATICAN COUNCIL, Dogm. Const. On the Church, *Lumen Gentium*, n. 13; cf. POPE JOHN PAUL II, Apost. Letter (Motu proprio) *Apostolos suos*, 21 May 1998, n. 22: AAS 90 (1998) 655–656.

Appendix

[61] Cf. *Code of Canon Law,* cann. 838 § 3.

[62] Cf. S. CONGR. FOR THE SACRAMENTS AND DIVINE WORSHIP, Letter to the Presidents of the Conferences of Bishops *De linguis vulgaribus in S. Liturgiam inducendis,* 5 June 1976: *Notitiae* 12 (1976) 302.

[63] Cf. *ibid.,* 300–302.

[64] Cf., S. CONGR. FOR DIVINE WORSHIP, Letter to the Presidents of the Conferences of Bishops *De normis servandis quoad libros liturgicos in vulgus edendos, illorum translatione in linguas hodiernas peracta,* 25 October 1973: AAS 66 (1974) 98–99; S. CONGR. FOR THE SACRAMENTS AND DIVINE WORSHIP, Letter to the Presidents of the Conferences of Bishops *De linguis vulgaribus in S. Liturgiam inducendis,* 5 June 1976: *Notitiae* 12 (1976) 300–302.

[65] Cf. S. CONGR. FOR DIVINE WORSHIP, Letter to the Presidents of the Conferences of Bishops *De normis servandis quoad libros liturgicos in vulgus edendos, illorum translatione in linguas hodiernas peracta,* 25 October 1973: AAS 66 (1974) 98–99; S. CONGR. FOR THE SACRAMENTS AND DIVINE WORSHIP, Letter to the Presidents of the Conferences of Bishops *De linguis vulgaribus in S. Liturgiam inducendis* 5 June 1976: *Notitiae* 12 (1976) 300–302.

[66] Cf. S. CONGR. FOR DIVINE WORSHIP, Norms *De unica interpretatione textuum liturgicorum,* 6 February 1970: *Notitiae* 6 (1976) 84–85; cf. S. CONGR. OF RITES, Instr. *Inter Oecumenici,* n. 40 c: AAS 56 (1964) 886.

[67] Cf. S. CONGR. FOR DIVINE WORSHIP, Norms *De unica interpretatione textuum liturgicorum,* 6 February 1970: *Notitiae* 6 (1970) 84–85.

[68] Cf. *ibid.,* 85.

[69] Cf. SECOND VATICAN COUNCIL, Const. *Dei Verbum,* n. 22; *Code of Canon Law,* can. 825 § 2; PONT. COUNCIL FOR PROMOTING CHRISTIAN UNITY, *Directorium Oecumenicum,* 25 March 1993, nn. 183-185, 187: AAS 85 (1993) 1104–1106; cf. *Code of Canons of the Eastern Churches,* can. 655 § 1.

[70] Cf. CONSILIUM "FOR THE IMPLEMENTATION OF THE CONSTITUTION ON THE SACRED LITURGY," Letter of the President, 16 October 1964: *Notitiae* 1 (1965) 195; POPE PAUL VI, Address to translators of liturgical texts into vernacular languages, 10 November 1965: AAS 57 (1965) 969; S. CONGR. FOR DIVINE WORSHIP, Norms *De unica interpretatione textuum liturgicorum,* 6 February 1970: *Notitiae* 6 (1970) 84–85.

[71] Cf. S. CONGR. OF RITES, Instr. *Inter Oecumenici,* n. 23 c: AAS 56 (1964) 882; *Code of Canon Law,* cann. 94, 117, 120; Cf. POPE JOHN PAUL II, Apost. Const. *Pastor Bonus,* 28 June 1988, art. 65: AAS 80 (1988) 877.

[72] Cf. POPE JOHN PAUL II, Apost. Letter *Apostolos suos,* 21 May 1998, nn. 18-19: AAS 90 (1998) 653–654.

[73] Cf. POPE PIUS XII, Encycl. Letter *Mediator Dei,* 20 November 1947: AAS 39 (1947) 561–562 ; SECOND VATICAN COUNCIL, Const. *Sacrosanctum Concilium,* nn. 44-46; POPE PAUL VI, Apost. Letter *Sacram Liturgiam:* AAS 56 (1964) 141; S. CONGR. OF RITES, Instr. *Inter Oecumenici,* nn. 44-46: AAS 56 (1964) 886–887.

[74] *Code of Canon Law,* cann. 333, 360; POPE JOHN PAUL II, Apost. Const. *Pastor Bonus,* 28 June 1988, art. 62-65: AAS 80 (1988) 876–877; cf. S. CONGR. FOR DIVINE WORSHIP, Letter to the Presidents of the Conferences of Bishops *De normis servandis quoad libros liturgicos in vulgus edendos, illorum translatione in linguas hodiernas peracta,* 25 October 1973, n. 1: AAS 66 (1974) 98.

[75] Cf. Congr. for Divine Worship and the Discipline of the Sacraments, Instr. *Varietates legitimae*, 25 January 1994: AAS 87 (1995) 288–314.

[76] Cf. *ibid.*, n. 36: AAS 87 (1995) 302.

[77] Cf. Missale Romanum, editio typica tertia: *Institutio Generalis*, n. 398.

[78] Pope John Paul II, Apost. Letter *Dies Domini*, 31 May 1998, nn. 40, 50: AAS 90 (1998) 738, 745.

[79] Cf. *Code of Canon Law*, can. 838 § 2.

[80] Cf. *ibid.*, can. 838 § 3.

[81] S. Congr. for Divine Worship, Decl., 15 May 1970: *Notitiae* 6 (1970) 153.

[82] Cf. *Code of Canon Law*, can. 826 § 2; cf. also below, n. 111.

[83] Cf. Second Vatican Council, Const. *Sacrosanctum Concilium*, n. 122; S. Congr. of Rites, Instr. *Inter Oecumenici*, n. 40 e: AAS 56 (1964) 886.

[84] *Code of Canon Law*, can. 826 § 3.

[85] Second Vatican Council, Const. *Sacrosanctum Concilium*, n. 63 b; S. Congr. for Divine Worship, Decl. *De interpretationibus popularibus novorum textuum liturgicorum*, 15 September 1969: *Notitiae* 5 (1969) 333–334.

[86] Cf. Pope Pius XII, Encycl. Letter *Mediator Dei*, 20 November 1947: AAS 39 (1947) 561–562 ; Second Vatican Council, Const. *Sacrosanctum Concilium*, n. 45.

Appendix

Index

Agobard, Bishop of Lyon, 47–48
allegorical exegesis, 37, 106
ancient languages, 23–30
Ancrene Riwle, 80
"And with your spirit," 93–95
Anglo-Saxon, 72–73
Anselm of Laon, 98–99, 119, 120
archaic language, 101–06
Augustine, St, 33, 68, 108–09

Barfield, Owen, 101, 102
Benedicamus Domino, 85
Benediction, 115–16
Beowulf, 77
Bibles
   King James, 93
   Lollard, 90–91
   Nova Vulgata Editio, 32–36, 52
   Rheims Douay, 92–93
   Septuagint, 29–30
   Vetus Latina, 49
   Vulgate, 29–30, 32–33, 49, 50, 52
   See also Psalters, Scriptures
Blake, William, 102–03, 107
Book of Common Prayer, 93
Byzantine rite, 27, 51

Caedmon, 77–78
calendric terminology, 71–72
carols, 81–87
"Catholic," 119–20
Catholic Biblical Association, 10 n 2
Chaucer, Geoffrey, 80–81, 90, 96
Chinese rites controvesy, 64–65
Clement VIII, Pope, 50–52

Code of Canons of the Eastern
   Churches, 13
Congregation for Divine Worship, 9,
   21, 22
contact linguistics, 70–73
Coptic rite, 27
Creeds
   Apostles', 21–22
   Nicene, 18–21

diversi, sed non adversi, 20, 30
diversity/adversity, 37, 46, 51–52, 59,
   99, 109, 120

Eastern rites, 13–14
Egeria, 25
embolism, 41
Emerson, Ralph Waldo, 101
Ethiopic rite, 27

friars, 89

Gallican rite, 11, 46–47
Gelineau, Joseph, 53, 110
General Instruction on the Liturgy, 26,
   114 n 203
Gray, Thomas, 101
Gregorian chant, 28, 33, 49, 64, 77
Gregory the Great, Pope, 15–17, 50,
   95, 106–09
Guéranger, Prosper, 12

hagiological typology, 45, 46, 106
history, 96, 118–19

Hovda, Robert W., 116
Hugh of St Victor, 40

Ignatius of Antioch, 120
inclusive language, 10, 97, 105
inculturation, 9, 11–14, 55
  and tradition, 58–59, 62
Innocent I, Pope, 16 n 15, 62
Instructio Ecclesiastici Ordinis, 11–12
Isidore of Seville, St, 55

Jerome, St, 33, 44, 68
Jerusalem practice, 27–28

kinesics (movement), 109–18
Kyrie eleison, 24–26, 29, 30–31, 82–86

Langland, William, 80, 89
language
  change, 73–75
  contact, 70–73
  stratification, 68–70
"Latin," 71
"Latin Church," 11, 18
Latin songs, 78–79
"legend," 75
Leo the Great, Pope, 14–17, 18, 22 n 28
Leo XIII, Pope, 48
lewdness, 76, 82, 88
Lewis, C. S., 103, 109
litanies, 24
Liturgiam Authenticam
  absurdities in, 22, 95–96
  aggression in, 97–98
  principles, 10, 17–18, 23, 32, 39, 43,
    48–49, 53, 62, 76, 87, 93, 97, 105,
    117
  purpose of, 9, 65, 105
  spirit of, 52–56
  text, 123–65
liturgical exegesis, 33, 37
liturgical history, 118–19
liturgical ideals, 106–09
liturgical interpretation, 43–46
liturgy as text, 44, 112–27
  see also oral performance
Lollards, 90–91

Lord of the Rings, 104
Lord's Prayer, 41
Lyons, rite of, 47–48

Merton, Thomas, 58–59
Missale Romanum
  of 1570, 25, 45
  of 1604, 50–51
  of 2002, 22, 23 n 29
Mohawk, 64
Mozarabic rite, 11, 28, 63
Murphy, John L., 112 n 200
mystical body of Christ, 108

New Spain, 63–64

oral performance of Scripture,
  39–45, 49, 89

paralanguage (non-verbal sound),
  109–18
Parsch, Pius, 54
performance studies, 111
Piaget, Jean, 110–11
Pius IX, Pope, 48
"placebo," 74, 102
poetic language, 101–06
Polycarp, St, 120
Pontifical Biblical Commission,
  37 n 62
prosulae, 25–26, 30–31
proxemics (use of space), 109–18
Psalters
  Gallicanum (Vulgate), 33, 49
  juxta Hebraeos, 33, 37, 49
  Old Roman, 29, 33, 49
  Pius XII, 32 n 52, 34 n 55

rites
  Carthusian, 47
  Chinese, 64–65
  Eastern, 11, 13–14, 19, 24, 26–27, 63
  Gallican, 28, 46–47, 63
  Glagolithic, 24–25
  Lyon, 47–48
  Mozarabic, 19, 24, 28, 63
  Syriac, 64
  see also Roman rite

Roman rite, 11–30, 63–66
  as example of inculturation, 11–12
  historical development of, 17–30
  as instrument of inculturation,
    12–30, 46
  need for protection, 11, 14, 18
Rufinus, 22 n 28

Scripture
  additions to, 42–43, 56–57
  gender switch, 44
  interpretation, 43–46
  modifications, 41–46, 56–57
  oral performance, 39–45, 49
Scriptures
  Gen 3:15, 33 n 53
  Esther 13:8-11, 15-17 Vulg,
    [NAB 4C:1-4, 8-10], 45
  Ps 8:6, 35
  Ps 34 [35]:2, 86
  Ps 44 [45]:17, 35
  Ps 114 [NAB 116:1-9], 102
  Ps 117 [118]:25, 29
  Ps 138 [139]:17, 35
  Ps 138 [139]:18, 33-34
  Prov 2:3-4, 54
  Song 1:6, 56
  Song 6:11-12, 55
  Wis 18:15, 36 n 59
  Sirach passim, 56–57
  Is 6:3, 30
  Is 7:14, 38 n 64
  Is 40:3, 38 n 66
  Zech 13:6, 36 n 60

Matt 6:9-13, 41
Matt 20:30-31, 24
Mark 7:34, 30
John 3:8, 101
I Cor 13:12, 96
I Cor 14:23, 119
I Peter 5:1-3, 98
Semitic words, 29–30
Star Wars, 104
Syriac rites, 64

texts, 44, 112–27
  see also oral performance
Thomas Aquinas, St, 18, 19–21, 37
tradition, 58–59
translations, 9, 22–23, 32, 39, 46, 53,
    60, 66, 88
  use of ancient languages, 23–30
Trent, Council of, 25, 32, 50–51
trisagion, 26–29
tropes, 25–26, 30–31, 69
Tyndale, William, 49

Vatican II
  Dei Verbum, 100
  Gaudium et Spes, 60
  Orientalium Ecclesiarum, 13
  Sacrosanctum Consilium, 36
Venice, St Mark's cathedral, 60–61

Warshaw, Robert, 115
Wilfrid of York, St, 77

"Zipf's Law," 75